Unearthing London

The Ancient World Beneath the Metropolis

Simon Webb

The History Press

First published 2011

The History Press
The Mill, Brimscombe Port
Stroud, Gloucestershire, GL5 2QG
www.thehistorypress.co.uk

British Library Cataloguing in Publication Data.
A catalogue record for this book is available from the British Library.

ISBN 978 0 7524 6274 5

Typesetting and origination by The History Press
Printed in Great Britain
Manufacturing managed by Jellyfish Print Solutions Ltd

Contents

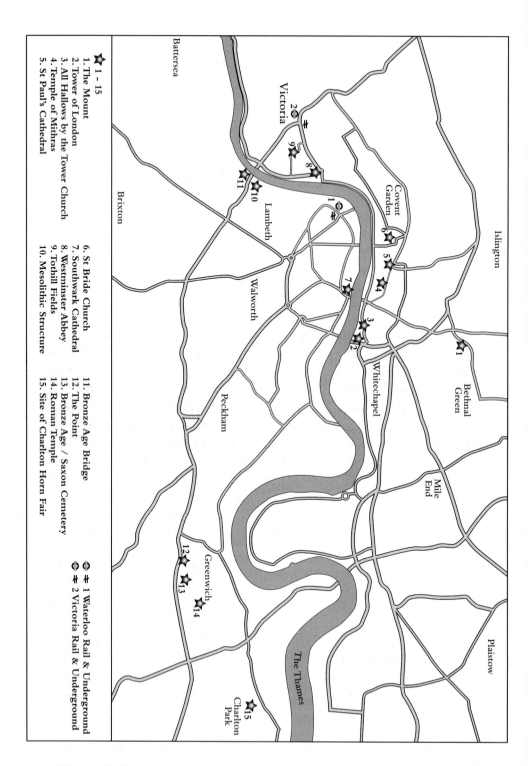

1 The principal London sites mentioned

1

Setting the Scene

It is a curious fact that while any educated person in this country is likely to be familiar with the ancient and mythological history of the Romans, Greeks and Jews, the legends and early history of his own nation will probably be completely unknown. Other cultures might have gods, heroes, kings and cities dating back a thousand years before Christ; we in this country have nothing more than vague images of cavemen and Druids. For most of us, British history really begins with Julius Caesar's landing in 55 BC. Even our capital city was supposedly established by the Romans, conventional wisdom holding that the area covered by modern-day London was more or less deserted marshland until the foundation of Londinium in about AD 45. A book published 30 years ago describes London before the Roman invasion like this: 'The Thames, much wider than it is today, flowed through an extensive and unhealthy marsh in which the only dry land was a few hillocks of gravel. The inhabitants of this forbidding swamp were a few tribesmen, water birds, fish and mosquitoes.'

Recent archaeological discoveries in the Greater London area have cast doubt upon this traditional image of prehistoric London. In 1993, for example, the remains of a wooden bridge or pier were found on the shore of the Thames at Vauxhall in central London. The timbers were dated to 1500 BC. The obvious question is who was building a bridge across the River Thames 3500 years ago and why were they doing so if nobody lived there except for water birds, fish and mosquitoes? More recently a far more ancient structure than this has been discovered, also on the Thames foreshore near Vauxhall Bridge: a group of wooden posts the size of telegraph poles, proved by carbon dating to have been erected over 6500 years ago.

Near Heathrow airport in West London, something even more surprising has been unearthed: an immense cursus or ceremonial causeway, 2½ miles long. This raised roadway was 6ft high, 60ft wide and has deep ditches on either side; it is roughly the size of a dual carriageway. Its construction would have been an enormous undertaking for a primitive society and it was built 5000 years ago. There may not have been a town or city where London stands today, but there were certainly enough people living nearby thousands of years before the Romans landed to carry out major civil engineering projects such as bridge building and the construction of raised roadways.

The evidence now emerging suggests that London before the coming of the Romans consisted primarily of a ritual landscape. What is a ritual landscape? This expression, coined by British archaeologists in the late 1970s, refers to a large tract of land with few inhabitants but containing many sacred structures such as mounds, barrows, megaliths, shrines and cursuses scattered across it. Salisbury Plain is a perfect example of a ritual landscape. The land there has been moulded and shaped into a complex arrangement of tombs and monuments which are still visible thousands of years later. This is such a strange concept today that it is worth pausing for a moment to think a little about the idea of a ritual or religious landscape.

In the modern world, with few exceptions, the overall landscape is wholly secular. Religious structures and areas tend to be small and self-contained. Churches, mosques, synagogues and graveyards are embedded within an irreligious background of streets, houses, shops, farms, factories, offices and parks. We have to make a special effort to hunt out our religious buildings. There is also a strict demarcation between the living and dead, with special patches of land called cemeteries or graveyards being allocated for the dead. These areas of the dead are almost invariably surrounded with fences or walls, both as physical barriers and as symbolic borders which emphasise the proper separation of the living and the dead. The situation in Britain before the coming of the Romans was often precisely the opposite. It was the landscape itself which was the religious backdrop. Human settlements were placed within this area and shared the land with the dead who were, in many cases, accorded greater respect than the living. In fact, the living and dead often coexisted amicably side by side. Sometimes corpses would be buried beneath or close to huts. Excavations have also revealed burial mounds which were raised over the remains of huts. In other words, a house containing a living neighbour would be replaced on his death with an earthen mound covering both his dead body and former home. Presumably, those living nearby would simply have accepted this, to us, bizarre and unwholesome arrangement! The massive causeway described above was quite possibly intended for the exclusive use of the spirits of the dead. The dead were housed in huge barrows and mounds, many of which are still impressive structures 3000 or 4000 years later. The living had to make do with poky, wattle and daub huts.

The idea that the Greater London area could have been just such a landscape is exciting for a number of reasons. First, a prehistoric cult centre where London now stands would tie in with many ancient British legends which have traditionally been dismissed by modern historians. The stories recounted by medieval chroniclers such as Geoffrey of Monmouth take on a new significance once we concede that London before the Roman conquest really did contain religious structures. For example, Geoffrey tells of temples in London before the Roman city was established. If rather than some classical stone building along the lines of the Parthenon, we interpret the word 'temple' loosely to mean a religious sanctuary or enclosure of some kind, then this story may well be true. Allowing for exaggeration, other tales of this kind might also have an element of truth in them.

That the area occupied by the present-day city might have been a cult centre is also intriguing because it means that we may be able to explore this ritual landscape and find traces of its existence. A number of barrows, wells and sacred places are still visible in central London, if one knows where to look, including an entire Bronze Age cemetery.

Another reason that the notion of London as ritual landscape is interesting is that it may shed light upon some of the most ancient folklore known to us. Evidence might be found for the worship of the horned god Cernunnos and his earlier avatars, as well as for the cult of the severed head and other, more obscure, practices. This also makes the early history of London worth studying for anybody with an interest in ancient mythology.

This book explores the thesis that London was an important place for those living in this country for at least 4500 years before the Romans built their city of Londinium. Archaeologists frequently have to travel to remote locations to verify their hypotheses. We are more fortunate; the city whose prehistoric and cultural origins we shall be considering is accessible and easy to visit. It will not always be possible to approach our investigation directly for two reasons. First, the society which existed before the Roman invasion was a pre-literate one. They left no written records and we are obliged to deduce their beliefs obliquely, by examining archaeological remains and the accounts of classical authors such as Julius Caesar. The pitfalls are probably at once obvious to readers. We may well misinterpret what we see and what a conquering army has to say of the primitive tribes which it feels obliged to subdue is hardly likely to be impartial. Often, we shall find ourselves viewing British history from the distorted perspective of those who thought it necessary to destroy or at the least irrevocably alter the customs which they found in this country. Archaeological finds are also likely to be seen from a distorted perspective; that of a largely irreligious society which places little value upon the numinous and divine.

The second difficulty to face us is that most of London is now buried beneath millions of tons of concrete, steel, stone, brick and tarmac. Traces are discernible of the ritual landscape which once covered the Thames valley in this area, but they are few and far between. We shall sometimes need to look at sites on the outskirts of the city, some of them 10 or 12 miles from central London. There is no cause to think that the temples and monumental prehistoric structures which are to be found on the edge of London are at all different from those which would once have existed in Westminster and the City. It is simply that these are lost to us forever and we must make the best of things by extrapolating from sites a little further along the Thames in either direction. This does not mean that the ritual landscape in central London has disappeared. It has rather changed and evolved; we must look for the later avatars or incarnations of the pre-Roman shrines and holy places which were once to be found on the river banks and hills of the capital.

A further difficulty with pre-Roman archaeology in the capital is that stone was not used as a building material. Wood and earth do not leave as many traces as masonry and when a section of Roman wall is found, it is not generally torn down by an archaeologist on the off-chance that beneath it will lie the faint marks of a Neolithic ditch or bank. With rare exceptions, the earliest physical remains in inner London are those of the Roman occupation.

The first and largely mythical accounts of London's history, which are found in manuscripts from the eighth century AD, may have their origins in folk memories from the Iron Age or even somewhat earlier. This provides a third source of information about prehistoric London, which we may use in addition to archaeological evidence and what Greek and Roman authors wrote about prehistoric Britain. Some legends were transmitted orally for hundreds, perhaps thousands of years before being written down. There are doubtless distortions and exaggerations in these stories, but we may sometimes discern, buried deep within them, nuggets of historical fact. The backdrop, though, against which characters of early British legends move was ancient even 2000 years ago. The grand age of barrow building and the shaping of ritual landscapes took place during the Neolithic period and Bronze Age, centuries before the birth of Christ. Even this is not the beginning of the story, because the Neolithic farmers themselves based their own belief system upon that of the hunter-gatherers who lived here before them. The roots of British folklore and mythology are buried very deep indeed in the distant past.

It is generally accepted that many old Christian churches were sited upon places which were formerly pagan places of worship. This served the double purpose of both supplanting the old religions and myth systems while at the same time ensuring a continuity of worship. Pilgrims came to the same places which their grandfathers had regarded as holy in order to pay homage to a new god. Indeed, this was officially sanctioned by at least one Pope. When Pope Gregory I sent St Augustine to Britain at the end of the sixth century in order to convert the heathen Saxons, he told him:

> Do not pull down the temples of the heathens. Destroy the idols and purify the temples with holy water, set relics there and let them become the temples of the true God. So the people will have no need to change their place of concourse and where of old they were wont to sacrifice cattle to demons, thither let them continue to resort on the day of the saint to whom the church is dedicated and

slay their beasts, no longer as a sacrifice but for a social meal in honour of Him whom they now worship.

What is not widely known is that this practice did not originate with the Christians. Romano-Celtic temples were sometimes built over older, wooden shrines. The Celtic Druids used megalithic temples for their own purposes, just as those who had originally built them had done so, because these locations were already regarded as sacred. So a Christian church might be built upon the foundations of a Roman temple to Mars, the god of war. This temple itself may have been erected upon the site of a Celtic wooden shrine which may have been raised over a Palaeolithic holy place in use over 10,000 years ago. This continuity of religious use of a particular location can be unbelievably long lasting, as the following instance will show.

The construction on Stonehenge is generally reckoned to have begun in the form of a ditch and bank in about 3000 BC. In 1966, though, during work on the car park, three postholes were found. These dated from the Mesolithic and indicated that huge wooden posts, each 2 or 3ft in diameter, had been erected near Stonehenge in 8000 BC. These could hardly have been part of a building; even the most primitive of buildings would need more than one wall! They were ritual structures of some sort. Five thousand years before Stonehenge was begun, this part of Salisbury Plain was already of great significance to the hunter-gatherers who lived in this country. Continuity of use, indeed; over 7000 years of attachment to one special spot on the plain.

This is not an exclusively British, nor even a European custom. The shrine of the Kaaba in Mecca, Islam's holiest site, was a place of pilgrimage for Arabs and Nabateans centuries before the birth of Mohammed. An even more ancient example is the Hala Sultan mosque near Larnaca in Cyprus. There, the mosque has actually been built around and wholly encloses a Neolithic trilithon, which is revered as marking the tomb of the Prophet's aunt. However, the megalithic monument predates the Muslim era by a couple of thousand years.

In Britain and the rest of Europe, this tradition of recycling a place of worship so that it accords with new religious sensibilities has been well established for many thousands of years. The Cathedral of Notre Dame in the French town of Chartres provides a perfect illustration of how the process works. Over 4000 years ago, there was a dolmen where Chartres Cathedral now stands. This consisted of three massive upright blocks of stone, topped by a third; rather like a scaled down version of Stonehenge. Nearby were a well and a mound. For reasons at which we can only guess, this was thought by the Neolithic inhabitants of this part of France to be an extremely holy place. Two thousand years after the construction of the dolmen, the Celtic Druids used the site as a sanctuary. They built a wooden temple here, which contained a crudely carved image of a goddess holding her child. Long before the birth of Jesus, they called this figure 'The Virgin under the Earth'.

In the third century of the Christian era, the blackened idol of the Druids was dug up by those building a church and it was named the Black Madonna. Four thousand years after it was used as a holy place by prehistoric farmers, Notre Dame in Chartres is still a place of pilgrimage associated with the cult of the Mother of God.

London has many examples of this continuity of use. The entire area of the Thames valley now covered by the city is a palimpsest, where scraping away at one layer of history or myth always seems to reveal another hidden beneath it. Some places seem to act as magnets for this sort of continuity. One of these is to be found on the south bank of the Thames.

The area around Duke Street Hill in Southwark, on the south bank of the Thames near London Bridge, has been used as a religious site for over 3000 years. A Bronze Age barrow was excavated here and in Roman times there was a well, where Southwark Cathedral stands today. A couple of hundred yards from the cathedral was an extensive Romano-Celtic temple complex. When the well beneath Southwark Cathedral was investigated in 1977, a cult figure was found at the bottom of the shaft. This stone statue was of a hunter god, accompanied by two dogs. It is probably a representation of Cunomaglos, the Celtic god known as the Lord of the Hounds. That this image should have been cast into the well in this way suggests a religious association; possibly that this was a so-called holy well and that the statue was deposited here as part of a closing ceremony when the well was filled in.

At a later date, 300 or 400 years later in fact, a church was built right on top of the old well. This is the church which later became Southwark Cathedral. A pagan site was thus superseded by a Christian one. Now wells and pools attract votive offerings, even today. There is something about a small body of water which causes people to cast coins into it while making a wish. This has been a common practice for thousands of years. Architects realise this and take it into account when they incorporate a pool into some public space, whether it be the foyer of a building or catchment basin of a fountain. It is simply a fact of life: passers-by will throw coins into such places while making a wish.

2 The statue of a hunter god recovered in 1977 from the well beneath Southwark Cathedral (*Tom Vivian, with kind permission of Southwark Cathedral*)

Further archaeological investigations at Southwark Cathedral a few years ago revealed a section of a Roman road and an ancient stone coffin. These discoveries, together with more recent gothic stonework, were left exposed for the public to see by leaning over a railing. They lie perhaps 10ft below the present ground level and one gazes down a shaft to view them. No sooner had they been opened to the public, than the tribute of coins began. The focus for these attentions seemed to be the coffin, which was soon being chipped and scratched by the shower of metal. Enough was enough, and a protective barrier of wire mesh was stretched over the whole area. It was also found necessary to put up a sign, asking people not to throw money down in this way. This coffin is shown in *colour plates 1a & 1b*. Ironically, the figure of the Celtic god stands immediately adjacent to this sign. It was, of course, itself a possible votive offering.

This one small instance demonstrates how powerful the customs which grow up around such sites are. After a break of almost 2000 years, as soon as the opportunity presents itself, the ritual practices emerge again, as though from the collective unconscious.

This continuity may also be readily seen with other of the capitals most famous buildings. St Paul's Cathedral is built upon or near to the site of a Roman temple complex which was probably dedicated to Diana, the goddess of the hunt. Her worship was bound up inextricably with the image of the stag, which was a sacred animal to the Celts, who almost certainly had a shrine or sanctuary on this spot before the Romans occupied the area. The stag was for the Celts the cult animal of Cernunnos, the horned god who later evolved into the devil of Christian mythology. The origins of this horned god, though, are to be found many thousands of years earlier than the Celts and before even the Neolithic era. In the cave of Trois Frères in the French Pyrenees is a famous Palaeolithic or Old Stone Age painting. It shows either a man dressed as a stag or some half-human god. This painting, known as the Sorcerer, is over 15,000 years old and generally supposed to represent a prehistoric shaman or medicine man. We shall see later that hundreds of ox, boar and deer skulls were unearthed during building work at St Paul's in the late thirteenth century. This ties in perfectly with Pope Gregory's advice to Augustine and tends to confirm that the summit of Ludgate Hill was indeed a place of pagan sacrifice. We thus see that another present-day religious edifice in London may have its foundations in a belief system dating back tens of thousands of years.

As we explore the early history of London, we shall be encountering some images again and again. The hunter, the horned god, the sacrifice, the votive offering; all these will be found in various locations across the city. We must begin by examining the topography of London and seeing why it was ideally suited to the role of cult centre. As we do so, we shall uncover a vast and intricate network of hilltop shrines, tracks, sacred rivers, mounds, ditches, enclosures and manmade hills, all well over 2000 years old. It is the city nobody knows; the hidden city which lies beneath the feet of its 8 million inhabitants.

Before starting, it might be as well to say a few words about the various periods into which British history is traditionally divided: the upper and lower
Palaeolithic, Mesolithic, Neolithic, the Beaker People, Bronze Age, Iron Age
including the La Tène Culture and Hallstadt, and so on. There are two difficulties
in following this nomenclature in a book of this sort. The first and most obvious
is that readers will be unable to visualise how long ago we are talking about and
what life was like at that time, unless they are either archaeologists themselves or
keep checking back to lists of dates, names, descriptions of Stone Age technology,
types of ceramics being used and various other things. Most people when reading books on prehistoric society have, unless they are enthusiasts for the period,
only the vaguest notion of the difference between the upper Palaeolithic and the
Mesolithic or Hallstadt and La Tène. All that we need know for the purposes of
this book is that the first people in this country wandered from place to place and
lived by hunting and that later on others began farming the land and living a settled existence. This, in brief, is the difference between the Palaeolithic, Mesolithic
and Neolithic eras. The settled farmers established themselves here around 3500
BC and this was the start of the Neolithic. Later on bronze, which is a mixture of
the metals copper and tin, was used to make tools and weapons, rather than the
stone which had been used for millions of years up until that time. Seven or eight
hundred years before the Roman invasion, people began to use iron instead of
bronze. This is, essentially, all that the average reader will need to know to make
sense of the arguments advanced in the present book.

There is another reason why it is not very helpful to emphasise these historical
periods. Until relatively recently, the prehistory of Britain was thought to consist
of a series of invasions, in which new cultures violently displaced the existing
order. This now seems unlikely. It is true that waves of immigrants from continen-
tal Europe periodically arrived in this country during the millennia preceding
the Roman occupation, but there is no reason to suppose that these were in any
real sense invasions. Britain was far less crowded than is now the case and most of
these newcomers would have been able to carve out farms and villages of their
own, without impinging upon the territory of the existing population. Any conquest would have been that of superior technology or different languages, rather
than force of arms.

A natural consequence of this is that religious belief did not change dramati-
cally from one prehistoric period to the next. It was not the case that one set of
gods was evicted and that other, foreign deities replaced them. As often as not,
the newcomers would adapt to the religious customs of the country in which
they settled. The reason for this is that their beliefs may have been broadly similar
in any case. The cult of the dead, the spirits living in rivers and wells, the special
position of the stag, the importance of the severed head, all these were common
to the whole of Europe and the Middle East. It was not the case that a Neolithic
farmer got up one morning and found that the Bronze Age had started during

the night and that his gods had been thrown down and replaced with a new set! Changes of technology and culture would take centuries to spread and differences would be subtle and elusive over the course of any one lifetime.

It is customary to draw a sharp distinction between, say, the Celtic Druids and those who built Stonehenge many centuries before Druidism was even thought of. This seems increasingly to be a false and misleading distinction. It is more helpful to see the Druids as a later manifestation of a religious tradition dating back at least 30,000 years and quite possibly longer than that. The story of religious belief in this country is not one of sudden and dramatic change, entailing the death of the old gods and wholesale adoption of the new. It is more a tale of gradual displacement and the transformation of men into gods and gods into men and women. We shall attempt to chart some of these changes, seeing how ancient shamans became horned gods, who in turn were transmogrified into devils and sometimes became men again. We shall see a mighty goddess who was demoted to mortality, becoming a Druid's daughter.

The main thing to be observed is continuity: the same London locations being used for broadly similar purposes by successive cultures and different religions. An ancient pre-Christian cult centre became a Romano-Celtic temple and then a Christian church; over the centuries, this church being transformed into a great abbey and a royal palace was built next door to it, before it finally evolved into the parliament building – the seat of government and legislature of the entire country. The story of London is the story of the same things being done in different ways and for various purposes in the same physical locations.

It is unlikely in the extreme that any large-scale archaeological digs will be authorised beneath the capital's main cult sites such as St Paul's Cathedral or Westminster Abbey. This means that we may have to look at other sites in the Thames valley and extrapolate from them to see what was probably happening in the London area at the same time. This approach throws up quite a few surprises. For instance, it is not generally known that a henge monument lies within the orbit of the M25 motorway.

A final word about terminology. In addition to avoiding the use of words like Mesolithic, I have also tried to avoid any obscure technical expressions which are unlikely to be familiar to the average reader. There are a few exceptions to this; three words which will be used fairly often and whose meaning might not be immediately apparent. Liminality is one of these words. I shall go into the precise meaning of this word in Chapter 2, but essentially it refers simply to the area where one thing changes into another. Votive, as in 'votive offerings', means giving something in exchange for the fulfilment of a promise or vow and an 'avatar' is simply the incarnation or manifestation, usually of a deity, but occasionally of a place or custom.

2

Rivers and Hills:
the Origin of a Ritual Landscape

London is a city of rivers and islands. This is difficult to appreciate today, because almost all the city's rivers apart from the Thames itself have now been culverted over and buried beneath concrete and tarmac. Nevertheless, over a hundred miles of rivers still flow through the city. They are remembered now chiefly in street names; the Fleet, for example, which flowed past Fleet Street and entered the Thames near present-day Blackfriars Bridge and Effra Road in Brixton, which follows the course of the subterranean river. *Effra* is a Celtic word which means 'torrent'. In addition to the Fleet and Effra, there is the Walbrook, the Tyburn, the Westbrook, the Neckinger, Falcon Brook, Stamford Brook, Ravensbourne, Quaggy River and several others. *Figure 3* shows some of the rivers of London which have now been lost to sight.

Rivers, lakes and wells were of enormous significance to the prehistoric communities of northern Europe; particularly those living in Britain and France, who were on the Atlantic coast of the continent. They were seen as entrances to the underworld, the land of the dead. These were the borders between the living and the dead and much of the religious practices in this country were, for thousands of years before the coming of the Romans, conducted whenever possible in the near proximity to natural sources of water. This idea, that rivers are in some way borders to the world of the dead, is deeply embedded in European folklore. We see it in Greek mythology, of course, with the River Styx marking the boundary between the land of the living and the realm of the dead. The Greeks did not invent this notion though; its origins lie a good deal further back than classical Greek mythology. The large number of rivers, streams, marshes and islands alone made the area of London an ideal focus for religious activity. It would, in a way, have been odd if London had not evolved into a ritual landscape during the Neolithic Age. It was not just their status as openings to the world below that made rivers of great importance to the men and women who lived in Britain thousands of years ago. They were seen as borders or boundaries in a far broader way.

Before we go any further, it would be a good idea to try and visualise the area that later became London. It consisted in the main of large tracts of marsh and fenland. These swamps surrounded many small islands, on a few of which were hilly mounds of dry land. Through the marshes and around the islands flowed many streams and tributaries of larger rivers which flowed into the Thames. Recent work has uncovered more and more little islands, which were found both on the edges of the smaller rivers, as well as in the middle of the Thames itself. A few of these larger islands still exist, at least upstream of central London. Eel Pie Island is one. There were other small islands in the middle of the Thames near Southwark and Westminster, but these have been swept away by the changes which have been made in the width and path of the river. The River Thames itself was once far shallower and broader than is the case today, so shallow in fact that at low tide it was possible to ford the river at Westminster. Because it was so wide and had no clearly defined banks, the ebb and flow of the tide had a greater effect than is now the case. Today, the only noticeable difference made by the tides is that the water level rises and falls against concrete and stone embankments. Before the Thames was contained in this way, the surge of the tide regularly inundated large stretches of marshland and fen. Islands disappeared entirely at high tide and low tide revealed mudflats and marsh. There was little truly dry land in what was later to become central London, which was little more than a vast, marshy floodplain. A few hillocks of gravel covered in brick-earth at spots like Southwark, Ludgate Hill, Cornhill and Tower Hill and that was about it. *Figure 4*

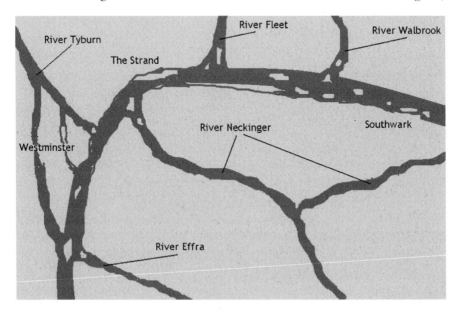

3 The rivers of central London as they were during the Bronze Age

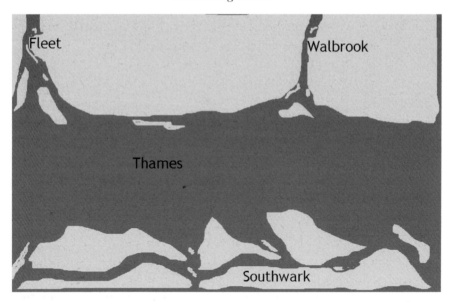

4 Central London at the time of the Roman invasion

shows the topography of central London 2000 years ago. It is as watery as Venice and even the spaces between the rivers are seldom truly dry land, but more often swamp. Islands, particularly the sort of small islands scattered throughout the area which became London, were, like rivers, seen as being somehow special in a religious and spiritual sense. It is time to outline the idea of liminality, a major factor in the development of the Thames valley as a ritual landscape and also one of the reasons that London came to be the capital of Britain.

Liminality simply refers to the transition from one stage or phase to another. This can be a physical change, an increase or decrease in status or a shift in time. It is also used to describe the existence of some thing or state on both sides of a boundary, whether spatial or temporal. Consider for a moment the transition from day to night. This does not happen in an instant. There is a period of time when light turns to darkness. We called this liminal zone 'twilight'. The boundary between day and night is thus not a sharp line, but rather a fuzzy area; the border is really an entity in its own right which is neither one thing nor the other. The spring and autumn equinoxes provide another instance of this. Before the autumn equinox, days are longer than the nights. The time of the equinox itself is neither one thing nor another; it is the time when the change occurs. This is not a moment, but a period of time. Beaches are another example of liminal zones. They mark the division between land and sea, but this again is not a sharp and clear-cut boundary. The waves lap to and fro, the tide ebbs and flows, and even when you paddle into the water, there is an in-between place where it is hard to say whether you are in the sea or on dry land. Shores, beaches, fords and natural river banks are by their nature liminal, as are swamps and bogs.

This is, of course, quite different from the way that we see liminality today. In our world, my neighbour's garden ends at the precise place that my own begins. There is no 'in-between space' at all, just a sharp and clearly delineated boundary. Farms and graveyards, gardens and housing estates, roads and rivers – all are clearly marked and measured today. This precision extends to time as well. One day becomes another at the very instant that the second hand touches the 12 on the clock. We seem to have abolished both spatially and temporally the spaces between places and times. The River Thames today has a distinct identity and we can mark its position on a map of central London to within a fraction of an inch.

This abolition of zones of temporal liminality is a fairly recent matter, dating back only a few centuries. Until the Industrial Revolution, with its factory shifts starting at exact times and railway trains leaving stations on the hour, work began at about dawn and might have ended at twilight. In farming, there is seldom any need for split second timing; the seasons are more important than the minute. In the same way, areas of land too were once delineated in a vague way. Today, everything must be timed to a fraction of a second and measured to a nanometre.

From a temporal perspective, zones of liminality may have diminished from the Industrial Revolution onwards, but as far as London is concerned, the curtailment and eventual destruction of the liminal shorelines and fens began with the construction of the Roman city, soon after AD 43. One does not want the tide to flow up and down streets or into houses and so the taming of the Thames began with the establishment of the first permanent buildings around the triple hills of Ludgate, Cornhill and Tower Hill.

There is plenty of evidence that the Neolithic and Bronze Age inhabitants of Britain were fascinated by this concept of liminality; the way that one thing became another and the indistinct, in-between zone where this happened. The transition zone between dry land and water seems to have been a special case of the phenomenon of liminality which was invested with supernatural and religious significance. Marshes, bogs and swamps were important because they were places on the very edge, neither dry land nor water. We shall see later that these are the sort of places where sacrifices of both material objects and human lives were made by our ancestors. The part of the Thames valley which is today Greater London was therefore ideally suited to become a centre of spiritual and religious life for those who lived in Britain thousands of years ago. We can see now why small islands were regarded with some awe. One is never far from the shore or zone of liminality on a small island. Indeed, if they are very small, they might be said to be almost completely liminal.

In the next chapter, we shall look at the way that the secular and the religious were not sharply delineated in prehistoric Britain. As far as London is concerned, this resulted in the liminality of this part of the Thames valley being of both religious and political importance. To see why, let us look first at the role of the River Thames as a border between rival British tribes in the years leading up to the Roman invasion. North of the river are the Catuvellauni and across the river is the territory of the Atrebates – this is a very simplistic and misleading representation of the actual situation. In fact, the area on both banks of the Thames was a liminal zone, a transitional space between territories. There has often been speculation as to why a large settlement was never established before in the region where the Romans founded their city of Londinium. After all, the tidal river reaches this far, there is abundant fresh water, a ford to cross the river. It seems perfectly situated to provide a suitable location for a town or port. Viewed though as an in-between place, belonging to neither northern or southern tribes, this space serves a useful function, far more useful than as merely a commercial area to land goods from the continent, which was, of course what the Romans had in mind when they started a town here. The liminal zone extended from either bank, forming, in effect, a buffer of land between the tribes. Evidence from other parts of the country suggests that areas like this had their own rules and customs, quite distinct from the territories and groupings on either side. Remember that this is more than a borderline between two tribes or territories; it is also the border between the living and the dead, the ordinary world and the realm of spirits, the wet and the dry. Members of any tribe would treat such a place with reverence and awe. Looking at the river's edge itself, this would be composed of several liminal zones. There is the indistinct and varying region where the water laps against the land. This is constantly moving backwards and forwards with the tide; there is no fixed and definite division between river and land. This is also the dividing area between the world of the spirits and the world of the living and, since each river had its own deity, also the area between the mortal world and the realm of a divine being.

On a more practical note, this whole region on either side of a large river like the Thames would probably be a kind of demilitarised zone, where traditional enemies might meet without fighting. The use of weapons would perhaps be forbidden in such a place and it might have been neutral ground where people could meet to thrash out their disagreements. As such, this liminal zone could have served an exceedingly useful function. It would provide a space where everybody could meet safely, without the threat of violence hanging in the air.

The tendency for the districts alongside rivers to be seen as special or sacred was not restricted to the Thames, but was applied also to its tributaries. We shall shortly look in detail at one of these minor rivers, the Walbrook. This river flowed through the centre of the Roman city of Londinium, entering the Thames near Cannon Street station. *Colour plate 2* shows the Roman city, with the Walbrook passing through the middle. Due to the number of ritual deposits and other things found in and near this river, it has been suggested that the whole Walbrook valley was a religious district, with temples and shrines lining the river banks. This is an interesting idea, because this kind of tradition has a way of lingering on and manifesting itself in later cultures and religions. Holy wells and springs were often taken over by Christians and a number became the sites of religious houses in the Middle Ages. Along the Thames itself, large areas of the banks on both sides were occupied in the Middle Ages by various monastic orders; the district between Fleet Street and the river was divided up between the Dominicans, Carmelites and several other orders. The valley of the River Fleet was also lined with nunneries and monasteries, clustering around the holy well known as the Clerks' Well. The presence of religious districts of this sort can help us to identify prehistoric sacred sites.

Within the larger liminal zone which covered the area which is today London, there were probably official locations where discussions and meetings took place, rather like meeting halls or conference centres. One such centre now lies beneath the M25 road encircling London; there would have been others. This site is called a causewayed camp and it is a bit like a hill fort. It jutted out on a small peninsula or promontory, sticking into the River Thames. Being this close to the water and almost completely surrounded by the Thames would have made it a significant place, being almost entirely composed of liminal zone, somewhat like an island.

It will be observed that the extent of the liminal zone is indistinct and fuzzy. This would be reflected by the physical features encountered by travellers heading towards the river. On prominent hilltops, such as Primrose Hill in the north and Greenwich in the south, barrows would be seen. They would be clustered more and more thickly as the Thames was approached. These hilltops and the barrows upon them were outliers, indicating to the traveller that he was coming near to a special place. The closer one came to the Thames itself, the more signs would be seen of the special and holy nature of the land there.

Although it is accepted that no major settlement or town existed here before Londinium, it was obvious that travellers were expected and provision made for their journey. On both sides of the river in the east, including Silvertown in the north and Bermondsey, Greenwich and Thamesmead on the other bank, wooden trackways were laid down to enable travellers to cross the marshes. These have been carbon dated to 4000 BC, roughly 500 years before the building of Stonehenge. We shall look more closely at these trackways in a later chapter, but for now it is enough to say that despite there being no substantial settlement in the area of London, travellers were certainly making the journey there.

Not only were rivers seen as borders between two worlds, each river and well had too its own minor deity, roughly comparable to the Greek nymphs and naiads. These entities were able to grant wishes and help in various human enterprises and so gifts were made and petitions presented to the demi-gods who inhabited the river or spring. We talk facetiously now of 'Old Father Thames', but he was at one time the local god whose help and favour would be sought. This was part of the idea of the contract between the gods and men; a notion shared by the Romans, who found many of the religious practices in this country quite familiar when they settled here.

Put briefly, men made contracts or agreements with the gods. If the gods helped them to win a fight or punished an enemy with sickness, then a gift would be made to the river or shrine. For the Romans, religious observance was a matter of sticking to a bargain. The gods must be honoured and treated with respect. In return, they would help the nation which provided them with at least the form of worship. This was a matter of outward performance rather than personal belief. Elizabeth I famously remarked that she had 'no desire to make windows into men's souls'. She meant by this that as long as the outward proprieties were observed, she was not interested overmuch in what her subjects actually thought about religion. This just about summed up the Roman view of religion. If the appropriate sacrifices and rites took place, the gods would be satisfied. It mattered not a whit whether or not those conducting these ceremonies even believed in the existence of the gods to whom they were making the sacrifice. This was purely a business contract.

If rivers were borders between the living and the dead or portals to the under-world, then hilltops too were liminal zones where heaven and earth met. They served the same purpose as the 'High Places' mentioned so often in the Old Testament. London has few hills, but all that exist have in the past been used for various religious purposes. The few natural hills of the capital have been supple-mented by artificial mounds, some on the slopes of the existing hills and others built near to springs and wells. South of the river is the chalk escarpment of Greenwich and Blackheath. In central London at Southwark is Duke Street Hill, while on the other side of the Thames lie Ludgate Hill, where St Paul's Cathedral stands, Cornhill and Tower Hill. These hills are little more than gentle rises and one needs to go out a little further to Pentonville, Primrose Hill and Parliament Hill in order to find anything approaching a higher and more clearly defined hill.

In addition to these pre-existing features, a number of smaller mounds were built in the London area. The most famous of these was the Tothill, which was con-structed in modern-day Westminster. It has vanished now, leaving only a faint rise in the ground to show where it once stood (5). This was an example of a Toot Hill, of which more later. Another wholly artificial hill was Friars' Mount, which lay pre-cisely to the north of Tower Hill. The remnants of this are still visible and have been converted into a garden called Arnold Circus. *Figure 6* shows this mound.

Before looking in detail at subsidiary rivers and streams and the hills beside which they flow, we should first examine the single most important component of the landscape of London: the great river which flows through its heart. We have all heard of sacred rivers such as the Ganges and Jordan, but it seems strange to think that the broad, sluggish, grey Thames has also been a sacred river for thousands of years. Its very name makes it probably the oldest named geographi-cal feature in the whole of Britain.

The peculiar reverence in which rivers have been held in this country can be gauged by the astonishing persistence of their names. Towns can be called by many

5 The slight rise in the ground which is all that remains of the Tothill on Thorney Island

6 Arnold Circus, the old site of Friars' Mount

different names over the course of their history and nobody thinks anything of it. The ancient stronghold of the Catuvellauni in Hertfordshire was once known as Verulamion. The Romans changed this to Verulamium and later still it became St Albans. In the same way, Camulodunam switched names to Colchester; in both cases, this was a fairly routine and unremarkable procedure. Rivers however tend to keep their names for all time, albeit with occasional minor contractions over time – a letter dropped here and there. It is as though new settlers are wary of meddling with them and feel that it is safer policy to respect them by continuing to use their proper names. Because of this, the names of rivers in this country have remained unchanged for thousands of years. Some of their names are not only generally assumed to be pre-Celtic, but even in some cases pre-Indo-European. In other words, they are still called by names which had some meaning in languages which became extinct 5000 or 6000 years ago. The River Dee in Scotland, for instance, is probably named after the proto-Indo-European word *deva*, meaning god. This word is the root of the English word 'divine'.

The Thames is the most ancient British place name of which we can be sure, mentioned as it is in Caesar's writings. He refers to it as the Tamesis, which is virtually identical with the modern name. Further confirmation for the antiquity of the name is provided by a Roman potsherd from Oxford, which bears the inscription, '*Tamesubugus fecit*', 'Tamesubugus made this'. This name is conjectured to have been derived from the name of the nearby river. There has been much speculation over the years as to the meaning of the word 'Thames'. Some have suggested that it is derived from two Celtic words: '*tam*' and '*usighe*'. *Tam* means wide and *uisghe* means water, so the meaning of the name would be 'wide water'. Others believe that the name of the river is related to the Celtic words for 'dark'; the Irish word '*teimheal*' is from the same root. This would mean that the original name of the Thames simply meant something like 'dark river'.

The intitial 'th' in Thames only dates from the sixteenth century and has never been pronounced as anything but 't'. This spelling was introduced to give a classical air to London's river; it was thought that calling it the Thames, rather than the Tames, would make it look like a Greek place name.

The earliest recorded mention of the Thames is to be found in Julius Caesar's account of the invasion of Britain. Caesar first landed near Deal in Kent in 55 BC. This 'invasion' of 12,000 troops did not last long. The following year he returned with over 37,000 men and this time he meant business. After dealing with the tribes in Kent, he marched to London. It was here that he encountered the river which the local inhabitants apparently called the Tamesis.

How do we know that the Thames was regarded as a sacred river at the time that Caesar marched towards it? For many years, archaeologists have recovered the most fascinating artefacts from the Thames. Some of them, such as the Battersea bronze shield, now in the British Museum, are stunning examples of Celtic artwork. It had been thought at one time that these shields, helmets and other bronze items had simply been lost in the river, but the vast numbers involved make this seem unlikely. The Battersea shield is one of the finest pieces of Iron Age Celtic artistry known. It is inconceivable that the owner of such an item would, upon seeing it fall into the Thames, simply shrug and say, 'Oh well, never mind'. The same is true of the other shields, helmets and pieces of bronze-work which the Thames has yielded up in such numbers. The huge quantity of bronze objects which has been recovered from rivers and lakes in both this country and Europe makes it almost certain that the majority had been deposited intentionally in the water. Another clue is that most of these weapons and tools are unused. Some of the swords and spearheads recovered from water have been deliberately damaged or dismantled, while others have been partially melted in forges. The obvious conclusion is that all this bronze has been cast into the river as sacrifices or offerings either to the gods or the spirits of the dead. The sheer amount of bronze abandoned in this way has led some archaeologists to speculate that the mining of the copper and tin used in the alloy of bronze was itself a religious activity; that those mining it knew perfectly well that much of what they so painstakingly extracted from the earth would ultimately be buried with the dead or cast into the water as a sacrifice. This too ties in with the concept of the ritual landscape, that even so mundane an occupation as copper mining would be part and parcel of a religious lifestyle.

These offerings are typically found in special places, locations which have some religious significance for those prepared to hurl their portable wealth into the depths of a river or lake in this way. This is the case with the finds from the Thames. That they are not evenly scattered along the length of the river, but are rather concentrated in certain spots, shows that particular parts of the river were, at least from the time of the Bronze Age, especially holy places.

What of the name of the city itself? One of the first people to try and explain the derivation of London's name was Geoffrey of Monmouth. In his *Historia Regum Brittaniae*, he set forth the names of various supposed kings of Britain. One of these was Lud. Geoffrey claimed that the whole city was known as Caerlud or Lud's town. Over the years, this became corrupted to Caerlundein and then London. It has to be said at once that there is not a speck of evidence on either archaeological or etymological grounds for accepting this explanation!

Another explanation which has been advanced is that London is a contraction of the Celtic/Welsh Llyn Din, meaning 'lake fort'. In the nineteenth century the idea was mooted that Llan Dian was more likely – temple of Diana, based upon the likelihood of such a temple having once stood on Ludgate Hill. Perhaps the Celtic word *luund*, meaning 'marsh', is connected with the case. More recently, the original name of Plowonida has been put forth, being based upon the Indo-European roots of *plew* for swimming and *nejd*, relating to 'flow' and found in several European river names. This would give London a name meaning something like 'swimming river', based upon the fact that it was too deep to ford.

We will never know for sure, but very fact that the city 'Londinium' was established upon the Celtic region of the Thames valley called by something which sounded a bit like 'London' tells us though that *something* was here before Caesar arrived with his army.

The Thames is fed by many tributaries, some of which, as we have seen, enter the river in London. The Thames may have been the sacred river, but these other streams and rivers were also treated with respect by those who lived there thousands of years ago. One small stream which seems to have exercised a strong influence in this way is the Walbrook. This river rises at several sources near the districts of Shoreditch and Moorgate. One of these sources was near a holy well where an Augustinian priory was later built. It is right by the prehistoric mound known as Friars' Mount in Shoreditch.

The Walbrook is, in a way, an archetypal minor sacred river. Its source is a spring bubbling from the earth near a holy well. By this well was an ancient, manmade hill. A Christian religious body took over the area and claimed both the well and the mound as their own. Along its length, churches and temples have been sited for thousands of years. The temple of Mithras, seen in *colour plates 3 & 4* and excavated in 1954, stood on the banks of the Walbrook. Churches too are to be found above its course. St Stephen Walbrook is right next to the Walbrook, while St Margaret Lothbury was built on vaults which actually span the river. A number of important buildings are placed directly above the Walbrook; for example, the Bank of England and Mansion House. During building work on the Bank of England in the nineteenth century, the Walbrook was seen flowing beneath the foundations of the bank.

Intriguing evidence for the idea that the Walbrook was a sacred river is to be found in the excavations carried out by the famous archaeologist Augustus Pitt Rivers during the 1860s. Scores of human skulls, but no other bones at all, were found in the river bed. The Celts were, of course, enthusiastic head-hunters and these were almost certainly heads which had been lopped from their enemies and cast into the river as offerings to the gods. The discovery of the skulls in the Walbrook shows that not all Geoffrey of Monmouth's tales are made up. He wrote of a battle in London during which a group of Romans were captured by their enemies, who decapitated them and threw their heads into the Gallobroc. Gallobroc is an early name for the Walbrook. Some modern historians think that the skulls found in the Walbrook were deposited there during the destruction of the city by Boudica in AD 60. If so, they may very well be the decapitated heads of captured Romans. This suggests that even while we treat Geoffrey's mythological accounts cautiously, there may be buried within them at least some authentic folk memories of early British history.

The evidence for the Walbrook being a sacred river is not limited to the human skulls which have been recovered from its bed. The Walbrook flowed through the heart of Roman Londinium. Its very name is derived from the fact that it passed under the city wall: the Wall Brook. For the Romans and Romanised Celts living within London's walls, this stream would have been an ideal place to offer sacrifices and make bargains with the gods. Many coins have been found in the Walbrook and also lead tablets bearing inscriptions in Latin. These are typically curses and pleas for help from the gods and seem to have been an exclusively British idea; at any rate, they are almost unknown in the rest of Europe. The Walbrook served as a kind of post-box, a way of sending messages to the gods and also forwarding payment for services rendered. The tradition of throwing coins into a wishing well is a lingering folk memory of this practice. The suggestion has been made by some archaeologists that the banks of the Walbrook formed a kind of 'temple district' for Londinium; this is where the citizens came to make offerings and pray to their various gods.

It is in the nature of rivers to flow near and between hills. The valleys between hills have often been carved by rivers and so we would expect them to be associated with each other. Ludgate Hill, the site of St Paul's Cathedral, lies between the Walbrook and Fleet. The source of the Fleet is near Parliament Hill. The Tyburn passes close by Primrose Hill; the high ground at Greenwich is skirted by the curiously named Quaggy River. This close connection between rivers and hills seemed to be pleasing to the earliest inhabitants of London.

We have looked a little at rivers and seen that they had a religious significance to those who lived in this part of the Thames valley thousands of years ago, but what of the hills of London? Can we say anything of how they were viewed in ancient times? There are some clues.

The hills of London share a number of common features from an archaeological point of view. To begin with, they seem to have been popular places for burials and interments. There are many Bronze Age barrows on Greenwich Hill and a barrow from the same period was excavated on the slope of Duke Street Hill in Southwark, a stone's throw from London Bridge. On Tower Hill, the remains of a Bronze Age burial of cremated human remains was found and, during the digging of the foundations for St Paul's Cathedral, Christopher Wren noted that many coffins were unearthed which seemed to date from the Roman period and even earlier. Further out from the centre of London, Primrose Hill was once known as 'Barrow Hill' because of the number of burial mounds to be found on its slopes. At Parliament Hill near Hampstead is a prehistoric burial mound known as Boudica's Mound.

In addition to being used for burials, there are other curious features of London's hills. Two of them, Greenwich Hill and Pentonville, have caves at their summits. This is surprising, as London is not generally known for its caves. Caves, just as rivers, were also seen as entrances to the underworld. At Greenwich, an extensive system exists beneath a chalk escarpment known as the Point. It is claimed that so many caves and tunnels are to be found here that it would be possible to cross from one side of Blackheath to the other without coming to the surface. Whether this is true or not, it is definitely the case that the area is honeycombed with caves. In 2002 a hole 30ft in diameter suddenly appeared on Blackheath and there have been many similar occurrences in the past.

It is only a short walk from the caves under the Point to the Royal Observatory. During the nineteenth century, Jack Cade's caverns, as they were known, were a popular night club for the Victorians. They acquired a somewhat unsavoury reputation and, following the death of a young girl, were sealed up until the outbreak of the Second World War. It was hoped that they could be used as air-raid shelters, but after a brief exploration, nothing came of the plan and they were once again closed up. On one wall in these caves is a carved representation of a horned god, suggesting that at one time they were used for religious purposes. A short distance from Jack Cade's caverns are the remains of a Romano-Celtic temple complex. This too suggests that this hill had some sort of significance in ancient times.

The other cave is in Pentonville and was from a very early time known as Merlin's Cave (*colour plate 5*). It is only a stone's throw from the Angel tube station and some years ago was converted into a reservoir, which function it served for many years. The association of this place with Merlin is curious. Places with a magical or pagan association sometimes have Merlin's name attached to them in this way.

Something else which the hills of London have in common is that at least four of them were the sites of mazes. A maze stood by Tothill in Westminster and another was to be found near Merlin's Cave at the hilltop of Pentonville. At Greenwich, the traces of a turf maze can still be discerned in dry weather as a crop mark; the road running alongside Greenwich hill is called Maze Hill. In the sixteenth century there was a maze in Southwark, right next to Duke Street Hill. What could the significance of these mazes be? In Chapter 8, we shall look in detail at the various possible explanations for the presence of mazes by or on four of the hills of central London.

The final point to be made about these hills is the extent to which they became associated with places of Christian worship after the Roman occupation. This suggests that they were already in use as religious sites during and, most probably, before the existence of Londinium. On the summit of Ludgate Hill stands St Paul's Cathedral (*colour plate 6*). On Thorney Island, near to the old Tothill, is the Abbey of St Peter, more commonly known as Westminster Abbey, while alongside Duke Street Hill in Southwark stands Southwark Cathedral. In the case of St Paul's Cathedral and Southwark Cathedral, there is direct archaeological evidence to support the belief that the areas around these hills were pre-Christian places of worship. We shall look in Chapter 5 at the survival of pagan rites at St Paul's; practices which lingered on until the sixteenth century. At Southwark, a discovery was made in the seventies which makes it almost certain that this part of London was a place of pilgrimage before the Christian era. Excavations beneath the cathedral uncovered an ancient well. At the bottom of this shaft was found a statue of a British god in the form of a hunter with two dogs, probably Cunomaglos or the Hound Prince, a British deity sometimes linked to Apollo. This find ties in neatly with the Romano-Celtic temple complex uncovered a short distance away in Tabard Square.

We have seen that the topography of London has in the past been invested with a good deal of mystical meaning and that religious practices based around rivers and hills have been an established part of life here for thousands of years; since before the coming of the Romans, in fact. It is a curious to note the role of the rivers and hills in the planning of the city we know today. A number of buildings are positioned so that they have a close proximity to the Walbrook. The official residence of the Lord Mayor of London, Mansion House, is built directly above this river, as is the Bank of England. Several churches have also been built so that they are right over this river. The Tower of London, the most ancient fortress in the country, is situated next to the Thames, on the slope of Tower Hill. On the summit of Ludgate Hill stands St Paul's Cathedral. Buckingham Palace was placed so that it straddled the Tyburn river. Time, as well as longitude and latitude, are measured throughout the whole world from the Royal Observatory which sits at the top of Greenwich hill, a stone's throw from both the Romano-Celtic temple and Jack Cade's caverns.

All this means that the ritual landscape of ancient London has not wholly been obliterated, at least not in the central area. Ironically, despite the 2000 years of building on the rivers and hills which made this landscape, it is sometimes more visible than in outer areas. A perfect example of a causewayed camp, an important ritual meeting place, was, for example, found near Staines in 1961. It has subsequently been lost forever, buried beneath the M25 motorway. This type of complete destruction has seldom occurred in London itself. It is true that the earth banks, ditches and mounds are no longer generally visible nor, with one or two exceptions, are the temples and shrines. Nevertheless, their presence can often be deduced by looking at the current layout of the city.

The ritual landscape of London has not been lost; it has instead mutated and can still be seen today, albeit in a somewhat different form. The sacred rivers are still visible, even though they sometimes appear as no more than slight dips in a modern road. Sometimes it is possible to view them directly, through a grating in the cellar of a building. The prehistoric cult centres were replaced by Romano-Celtic temples, which in turn gave way to Christian churches. We can trace the continuity of use in some London sites for thousands of years in this way. The clustering of religious establishments along the Thames at Southwark and in the region of Fleet Street, Clerkenwell and Westminster allows us in this way to find the world beneath – the lost religious backdrop of Neolithic and Bronze Age London.

Perhaps the best example of this clustering of important institutions in London, both secular and religious, by rivers or near hills is to be found in Westminster. At some time in the past, certainly before the Roman invasion, a Toot Hill was erected near to where Westminster Abbey now stands. This mound was placed in a spot bounded by two branches of the Tyburn and the Thames itself. What is a Toot Hill? The plain answer is that nobody really knows. Toot Hill is the name given throughout Britain to various manmade hills and mounds. Some have suggested that they are lookout posts, others that they had some religious significance. It was Alfred Watkins in *The Old Straight Track* who noticed that along the line of the leys which he plotted were quite a few hills which included the word 'Toot', 'Tot' or 'Dod' in their names. In his translation of the Bible, Wycliffe translates a verse from Isaiah as, 'Up on the toothil of the Lord I am stondethe'. In the King James version, this is rendered as 'watchtower'. In London, the variation 'Tot' has come into use and the mound erected by the Thames in the modern district of Westminster was the Tothill, although the earliest writers do refer to it as the Toote Hill or Tuttle.

Certainly the Toot Hill at Thorney Island in London had some purpose or meaning beyond that of simple lookout post. After all, this island went on to become the site of not only Westminster Abbey, but also the Houses of Parliament, the very seat of government. Chapter 4 looks in greater detail at Westminster and its role in the creation of modern London.

Before we can hope to make any sense of the ancient landscape of London, we must try and see things from the point of view of the Neolithic farmers and Bronze Age warriors whose monuments and religious beliefs did so much to shape the early city. It is time to examine the ancient religion of the British Isles. Before we learn about the individual gods and goddesses who were worshipped in this country thousands of years ago, we must try to understand the mindset of these early Britons, because the way that they viewed religion and the supernatural was completely different from how these matters are generally treated in the modern, industrial West.

3

The Religious View in Ancient Britain

Before examining in detail the mythology and religious beliefs of the men and women who lived in London thousands of years ago, it is necessary to bear in mind that they operated from an entirely different perspective to us about such matters. There was, as suggested above, no sharp division between the sacred and the profane, no demarcation to separate secular from religious. The early inhabitants of the fertile river valley which would one day become London shared their world with the spirits of the dead, various gods and goddesses and also a number of supernatural beings of the sort that we would these days describe as fairies or elves. These other entities were not merely vague superstitions or matters only to be considered on special occasions or in particular places, as is so often the case with modern-day religious observance, but rather a real and integral part of their everyday lives. The ritual landscape was an expression of this mindset: that some of the dead should be housed properly and accorded at least as much respect as the living and also that the gods should be held in awe and placated by tribute. Much of the energy of Neolithic and Bronze Age societies in Britain was devoted to projects which would ultimately benefit only the gods and the dead.

Not only was surplus energy, the time and leisure left after the necessities of life had been procured, put into ritual observance, but also a great part of the material surplus: mined flint and metal, agricultural produce and manufactured goods. Gifts to the spirits were not a grudging or reluctant duty but the very business of life. Today, building a bridge or road is simply an awkward and time-consuming project which we wish to get finished as quickly and easily as is humanly possible. For those constructing a henge or cursus, though, the very work was a part of both their physical and spiritual life.

This has created quite a bit of confusion over the years among those who investigate the prehistory of this country and led to the regular misunderstanding of the nature of discoveries. Unless one puts oneself into the place of a Neolithic farmer and tries to view the world from his perspective, many of the activities which he undertook, the traces of which are uncovered during archaeological excavations, will be utterly incomprehensible. For many years, large collapsed holes have been found in London which contain the remains of food and other material. Shafts like this exist at Enfield in North London. The conventional identification of such pits has been either to dismiss them as rubbish dumps or suggest that they might have been silos for food which were suddenly abandoned. It suggests that our ancestors were very timid, constantly abandoning their larders at the first hint of trouble. Holes like this are now believed to be ritual shafts dug in order to make contact with the underworld. At Swan Street in Southwark, one of these shafts was excavated. It contained pots full of the skeletons of dogs and other animals. There were also a number of individual skulls. This was manifestly not a well, nor yet was it a midden or rubbish dump.

Other examples of misunderstanding the thought processes of our forebears are to be seen when large hoards of bronze or gold are dug up or goods recovered from the bottoms of rivers or old well shafts. Again, it has in the past been common to see these discoveries through the point of view of a modern person. Obviously, if one buries a couple of kilograms of gold in the ground these days, one intends to return for it at a later date. In the same way, a silver spoon dropped down a well can only have been an unfortunate accident. Such interpretations as these are, it is now generally believed, very far from the mark. Our ancestors must have been very careless and incredibly forgetful if they were able to bury the entire year's output from a copper mine and then simply forget where they left it! That these depositions were definitely deliberate and not in the least accidental is indicated by the case of Armorica in France.

The pattern of deposition of bronze axe-heads and other implements in that part of Gaul once known as Armorica, forming part of present-day Brittany, is very curious. So many bronze tools and weapons were found that it seemed as though those manufacturing such items must have been working flat out simply to maintain the supply of axes to be lost or deliberately buried in the earth. This activity, of axes in particular finding their way into the earth, reached a crescendo in the seventh century BC. So far, an astounding 40,000 bronze axes have been found from this period. All were buried intact and apparently unused.

Chemical analysis of the bronze used to make the tools from Armorica revealed something which settled once and for all the question of whether this was carelessness on an industrial scale or a ritual activity. To harden copper and make it more durable, it is alloyed with 10 per cent tin. This forms the metal known as bronze. Many of the finds of axes in Armorica were of copper alloyed instead with a high proportion of lead. This would have made them very soft and unsuitable for any practical use. They had been made purely and simply for deposition. The mining of the copper and lead, together with the forging of the weapons and tools made of this alloy, was therefore an entirely religious activity in this part of

Gaul, with no expectation that any of the products of this industry would ever be put to any use other than that of symbolic abandonment.

Even activities which we would today regard as being wholly secular, such as mining, road building, agriculture and the construction of bridges, were subsumed to the ultimate end of religion. Recent discoveries in Turkey, on the edge of that part of the Middle East where settled agriculture began, have suggested that even the standard view of how agriculture became established might have been seen back to front. Since this has a bearing on the landscape of prehistoric London and the construction of monuments and shrines, perhaps we should look at the implications of these new ideas.

The traditional view of the building of large structures such as henges, megaliths, burial mounds and cursuses is that it was first necessary for agriculture to develop. The surplus grain harvested would then provide a workforce with food. Freedom from the need to hunt for food every day, combined with the effects of being settled in one place, would give people leisure to think about higher matters and also allow them time to create religious structures. This would partly be because they were settled in one spot and wished to impose their own culture and identity upon the landscape. In short, the agricultural lifestyle was responsible for the development of religion and its external signs such as temples and shrines. Looked at from this point of view, religion and the ritual landscape were really no more than a by-product of agriculture.

On a plateau in Turkey is a vast sanctuary. Over 300ft across, it is made of huge blocks of stone weighing between 10 and 20 tons each. These are carved with pictures of various animals and the whole site was once surrounded by a wall. It has been estimated that at least 500 people would have been involved in the construction of this sanctuary. The interesting thing about Gobekli Tepe is that it was built around 8500 BC, a thousand years or so before the arrival of agriculture in the area. The implications of this discovery are staggering.

To feed a workforce of 500, along with their families, would require a large amount of food. Since this enterprise took place during the era of hunter-gatherers, it must be the case that in addition to those labouring to build the sanctuary, another large body of workers was engaged in foraging and hunting, while the 500 were hauling those cyclopean blocks of stone up on to the plateau. It is likely that it was construction work of this sort which showed the advantages to this Palaeolithic community of settling in one place and producing their food, rather than collecting wild berries and hunting animals. In other words, it may well be that rather than a settled, pastoral life bringing about the construction of religious sanctuaries of this sort, it was religion itself which motivated men and women to settle down and become farmers.

We see now how religion has, from even before the time of the first farmers, been inextricably bound up with the everyday life of prehistoric people. The idea of a division between the holy and the mundane would simply not have occurred to anybody living in Europe or the Middle East 5000 years ago. This lifestyle, where religious observance and respect for the dead was an integral part of life, can be seen in the very first towns to be built as humans abandoned the wandering life of the hunter-gatherer and settled down to till the earth and domesticate animals. Two of the earliest towns of which we know are Catal Huyuk in Turkey and Lepenski Vir in former Yugoslavia. In these towns, which flourished between 8000 and 10,000 years ago, religious and domestic life were indistinguishable. At Lepenski Vir, every single home had, in addition to a hearth, an altar. At Catal Huyuk about a third of the buildings were temples or shrines. The present arrangement in our societies, where places of worship are widely spaced and scattered sparsely throughout the secular backdrop, would have been incomprehensible to the first town dwellers.

In order to see how this world-view was applied in a place like prehistoric London, I want to look first at one particular location, perhaps the most important place in prehistoric London, that of the area on the north bank of the Thames, occupied by the modern-day district of Westminster.

We have seen that an artificial mound was erected on Thorney Island, where the River Tyburn divided into a delta and its several streams entered the Thames. This mound was known as Tothill. Thorney Island is still very important; both Westminster Abbey and the Houses of Parliament were later built there. Buckingham Palace lies on the western edge of Thorney Island, having been built right above the Tyburn River. This marshy area and gravel island, surrounded by fens, was of huge significance to those who lived in Britain. According to Geoffrey of Monmouth there was once a temple here, perhaps dedicated to Apollo, and Roman remains have certainly been discovered. It seems likely that there was a Roman building, perhaps a temple, where Westminster Abbey now stands; this is, of course, the sort of thing which might indicate a site associated with prehistoric religion, especially since the spot is now occupied by an important Christian place of worship. In the nineteenth century, a Roman sarcophagus was dug up here and during excavations for the underground a couple of years ago, a good deal of material from the Bronze Age and Neolithic period was also discovered. Since Westminster is some considerable distance beyond the walls of Londinium, we must suppose that there was something special about this place in order for anybody to bother lugging a huge, stone sarcophagus here, at least 2 miles from the city gates. There was, after all, a perfectly good cemetery located just outside the walls of Londinium at Bishopsgate. The Neolithic and Bronze Age remains are also of interest. Clearly, Thorney Island was being used regularly at least 2000 years before the Roman occupation. The Romans and later the Christians simply took over an area which was already regarded as holy in some way.

The Tyburn divided shortly before flowing into the Thames, with three or four branches entering the Thames at different points ranging between the palace of Westminster and Vauxhall Bridge. I mentioned in Chapter 1 that a Bronze Age bridge or jetty was excavated here in 1993. This led from some point on the riverbank opposite Thorney Island, out into the Thames. For how far, we simply do not know. This might be a good point at which to consider a couple of the theories put forward to explain this structure. It was found at a point in the river where branches of both the Tyburn and River Effra flow into the Thames from opposite banks. When the Thames was a good deal broader, shallower and more sluggish than it is today after all the embankments which have confined it, there was probably an island here, composed of gravel which the two rivers had pushed into the centre of the Thames. It is likely that the bridge or pier which was erected here around 3500 years ago led to this island. It may have then have extended to the opposite bank of the Thames or it might on the other hand have stopped dead in the middle of the river.

Readers are probably scratching their heads at this point and asking themselves what possible purpose could have been served by a wooden structure of this sort which reached only half way across a river. Why would anybody go to all that trouble building a bridge and then stop before reaching the other side like that? One theory is that it could have been a quay or jetty, where boats were loaded and unloaded. Or it may have served quite a different purpose, one wholly unconnected with what we would today regard as the practical business of life. This brings us back to the idea of a religious lifestyle for the whole community. The building of this bridge was a huge and time-consuming undertaking for the scattered communities living near the Thames and yet it is quite entirely possible that it had no purpose at all that we today would regard as practical. It might help us to look at a couple of similar sites: one in England and one in Switzerland, where similar bridges or jetties have been discovered.

La Tène is a village on the north side of Lake Neuchâtel in Switzerland. It gives its name to the Iron Age culture which flourished in Western Europe during the last few centuries before the Christian era began. In the nineteenth century, a drought lowered the level of the lake and revealed wooden posts dating back over 2000 years. Some of these proved to be parts of a pier, while others were the supports of houses built above the water on stilts. Many swords were found in the mud of Lake Neuchâtel. They were remarkable for the fact that almost all of them showed no signs of wear. They had apparently been thrown into the lake brand new. There were also quantities of jewellery, shield bosses and other remains, including many bones both human and animal. No female ornaments or jewellery were found, which suggested strongly that these items were not simply lost or abandoned. They had been deliberately chosen by men and thrown into the lake.

At Flag Fen, near Peterborough, a causeway very similar to that found at Vauxhall was constructed at about the same time. Consisting of 60,000 posts driven into the mud, it led to a platform in the water, in the vicinity of which a quantity of bronze has been recovered. The purpose of this causeway or bridge was probably to allow people to cast offerings into the water. It is possible that this was also the reason for the construction of the bridge in London. One clue that this enigmatic structure may have had a religious purpose was that when it was built two bronze-headed spears were thrust deep into the mud beneath it. These were definitely not lost; there was not the least question but that they had been driven into the foreshore as some kind of sacrifice.

Entirely possible is that the Vauxhall Bridge both served to allow people to cross the river and at the same time make an offering to either the gods or the spirits of the dead. This is such a strange idea that we must consider it a little more deeply.

Today, any government proposing to construct, say, a roadway for the exclusive use of the dead, as was perhaps done at the Stanwell cursus in West London, would not be very popular. Nor would they be likely to meet with approval if plans were published to build a bridge over a river which stopped dead in the middle of the water. This is because we in the modern world are almost exclusively concerned with the needs of the living. We often pay lip service to religious belief and pretend to have a respect for the dead, but this tends to stop short at once if it seems that either the needs of the dead or our religious convictions are liable to interfere with our present convenience. Ours is a world of the living. We might bury a relative with a favourite piece of jewellery, but would stop short of placing all her worldly goods and money in the grave with her. We want them for ourselves. What further use would a dead person have for her car or television? In the same way, we might put a few pounds in the plate at a church service, but we would not offer our car or plasma screen. We have very clear ideas about the limits of our obligations to either our gods or our dead relatives.

From the time of the earliest modern humans, it was the custom to bury the dead, or at least some of them, with things that they might require in the next world. Everything from strings of beads to horses and slaves, chariots to bowls of food, swords to crowns, would be placed in a tomb with the corpse to ensure that the next life would be no less comfortable than this one. The more prosperous the prehistoric societies became, the more that the produce of the society would end up being buried in the earth. This applied equally to necklaces made from animal teeth in the Stone Age to entire chariots in the Bronze Age.

Side by side with this custom of providing the dead with material goods, was the practice of casting valued possessions into rivers, lakes and bogs. We cannot now know the precise motive for these sacrifices. They may have represented bargains with the local gods, offers of thanksgiving or a way of sending goods on to the world of the dead. These offerings might also have been a quid pro quo. The gods of the river and earth provided good things for the community and it was only fair to return the favour. Perhaps there was also an element of 'conspicuous consumption' involved. It might have been a way for some chieftain or nobleman to demonstrate how wealthy he was and how little he cared for his wealth. What is certain is that this was a very common practice from the earliest times in this country. In other parts of Britain, hoards of bronze and occasionally of gold were also simply buried in the ground and abandoned. This too seemed to be a deliberate act, rather than simply misplacing the metal. One collection found in Cambridgeshire weighed over 95kg. It has been estimated that this mass would be the entire output of one copper mine for five years. It is hardly likely that such an enormous amount of valuable metal was simply mislaid and forgotten. Just as with the artefacts thrown into rivers and lakes, this was part of some common purpose; those mining it knew that this would be the ultimate result of their labour. The same probably applied to the flint miners of the Neolithic, because vast quantities of worked flints have also been recovered from lakes and rivers. Dredging for gravel in the Thames during the nineteenth century brought up tens of thousands of such flints, all unused and as good as new. Just as with the bronze swords, helmets and shields, these show every sign of having been deliberately thrown into the water.

It is by no means impossible that we have an eyewitness account of a ritual deposition of weapons in this way. It will be recalled that according to legend, as King Arthur lay dying after the Battle of Camlan, he ordered his companion, Bedivere, to take his sword and hurl it into the nearby lake. This story has the ring of truth. Hundreds of swords have been recovered from rivers and lakes after being cast into them in precisely this way. That a dying king should command his sword to be thrown in a lake so that no other man could ever wield it sounds exactly like an authentic oral tradition. Even Bedivere's initial reluctance to dispose of the sword in this way sounds convincing. The Lady of the Lake has the characteristics of the local deities to whom many votive offerings were made from the Neolithic onwards. However it came to us, it is quite conceivable that in this haunting little anecdote, we have a genuine folk memory of a real incident which took place a thousand years before the birth of Christ.

In London, this custom of throwing valuable things into the water was very prevalent. Particular parts of the Thames and its tributaries were favoured for this activity; the lower valley of the Walbrook, London Bridge and Brentford, for example. Outstanding examples of Bronze shields, helmets, swords and spearheads have also been found in the Thames. These too were almost certainly cast voluntarily into the river as sacrifices of some kind. One of the ways that we can be sure that these are not simply bits and pieces which have been lost over the years is that, almost without exception, these weapons are in perfect condition. The axe heads and sword blades are not notched or blunted with use. Some have been deliberately bent or otherwise rendered useless, but they have never been used for their intended purposes. Some of these axes and blades are particularly attractive, looking as though they had been made for decoration rather than use. This is also the case with the most famous artefacts which have come from the Thames. The Battersea shield, a fantastic piece of Iron Age metalwork, would hardly have been hazarded on a battlefield. It was obviously made solely to impress. Whatever the ostensible motive for hurling it into the Thames, its sacrifice in this way must surely have demonstrated to any onlooker that the person surrendering such a beautiful and valuable item was rich and yet prepared to surrender his wealth without hesitation.

Near the site of the Roman bridge across the Thames, a little to the east of London Bridge, coins too are often recovered. It is assumed that these were thrown into the river from the bridge, although it has also been suggested that a shrine stood on the Roman bridge and that this resulted in the regular donations of coins and other articles at this location. This would have served the same function as the platform at Flag Fen and also the Bronze Age structure at Vauxhall. In addition to coins, parts of bronze statues have also been found here. The throwing of broken cult figures into rivers and wells in London was a well-established part of religious life during the Roman occupation. This custom continued for at least a thousand years after the end of the occupation. Along with flints, bronze weapons and Roman coins, many medieval pilgrims' badges have been found in the Thames. So many that it is inconceivable that they have simply fallen into the river and become lost.

This process can be thought of as trading with the spirits or the dead. The river provided people with water and lumps of flint which were washed up on the shore. In return for taking these things, a certain portion of what was manufactured was returned to the river in exchange. The water from the river was also used for softening antler and bone so that they could be more easily worked. It was therefore only proper that a certain proportion of the finished products should be returned to the river as a thanks offering for the use of the water or gift of the flint. It was a bargain between men and the spirits of the water, whether gods or dead ancestors. Every activity undertaken by prehistoric people – hunting, flint knapping, farming, mining and everything else – was a joint venture between man and the spirits. These invisible entities could make or mar any enterprise. We still have vague memories of co-operative ventures of this kind between men and the gods. There are lingering echoes of such beliefs even in Christian churches. At harvest time, congregations in this country still sing:

We plough the fields and scatter the good seed on the land,
But it is fed and watered by God's almighty hand.

Observe that *we* plough the fields and scatter the seeds, but that it is *God* who waters and feeds them. Agriculture is thus portrayed as a collaborative venture between God and man, both having their part to play. Singing the songs in this way in a special building dedicated to the gods, shows that we acknowledge this and are showing our gratitude. In return, we hope that the gods or God will continue to send the sun and rain which are necessary for seeds to grow. We see a similar theme in the gospels, when Jesus accompanies the disciples on a fishing expedition. Their efforts are only crowned with success in the so-called miraculous draft of fishes when God wills it. It is not difficult to transfer this notion to the prehistoric community, even when engaged in industrial activities like mining, metalworking and the construction of roads and bridges. This world-view has been the common one throughout the whole of recorded history and earlier. In a sense, our own insistence upon a sharp demarcation between the divine and the worldly is the aberration.

Looking once more at the offerings made to the gods of the river, even now a ritualised form of this takes place whenever a large ship is launched. From ancient times, when building and launching a ship it has been seen as necessary to gain the favour of the gods who dwell in the rivers and oceans. The Babylonians sacrificed oxen, other nations poured wine into the water. We in this country continue this practice by breaking a bottle of champagne over the ship and invoking God's protection upon it and those who sail in it.

There was also the concept of a contract, mentioned earlier, which is where we come to the matter of votive offerings. In the Christian and Jewish tradition, making a bargain with God is generally frowned upon. There are certainly cases where it was attempted in the Bible, but it is clearly not the way that the Lord wants his people to behave. Those who lived in prehistoric Europe had no such inhibitions. They would, in effect, draw up an agreement or contact with a specific god or goddess. As long as the deity fulfilled his or her part of the bargain, the supplicant would furnish the temple or sacred site with a specified amount of money, goods, statues or anything else which struck them as being an adequate reward for the god's help and assistance. These were called 'votive offerings'.

This 'contract' type of religion became very much the rule during the Roman occupation of London. Such agreements could be very specific. Many lead 'curse' tablets have been found in the Walbrook in London and also at other Romano-Celtic sites in London. During the work on the London Amphitheatre in the 1988, for instance, a curse tablet was found which invoked the help of the goddess Diana. On these tablets were scratched the full details of what was agreed between the supplicant and the god. One from Gloucester concerns some linen stolen from an individual called Saturnina. In return for Mercury's help in recovering the stolen goods, Saturnina promises to give a third of the linen to Mercury and a third to Sylvanus. An early example of a 'no win, no fee' style agreement! This sort of contract seems to have been an especially British custom; there is, at any rate, little sign of its being practised in this form elsewhere in Europe. This leads many archaeologists to suspect that the practice pre-dates the Claudian conquest and has its roots in a British tradition.

The 'contract' notion of religion lingered on and was even incorporated for a time into the Christian faith. In Catholicism, such contracts with God and the saints persisted into historical times. The sale of indulgences, a form of votive offering, precipitated the reformation during the sixteenth century. Medieval pilgrims' badges from those who had made the pilgrimage to Canterbury were often thrown into the Thames on the pilgrim's return. Since we know that some people made pilgrimages as a means of penance or supplication at that time, it is hard to avoid the conclusion that throwing the badges into the river in this way was a means of demonstrating that they had fulfilled their part of the bargain and that the contract was now at an end.

Here again, we see old customs appearing after a space of centuries or millennia. There is also the same continuation of use of geographical locations. Those making the pilgrimage to Thomas Beckett's tomb in Canterbury would often set out from Southwark. The Tabard Inn, which Chaucer cites as a meeting place for those going on this pilgrimage, is right by the site of a Romano-Celtic temple complex. The act of pilgrimage was often a contract. The pilgrim had promised something to God and sought a favour in return. It might be forgiveness for some sin or the very act of making the journey might be seen as payment for some benefit which the pilgrim felt that he had received. On his return, he cast the badge into the river as he crossed London Bridge. This showed that he had actually been to the place of pilgrimage and that the contract had now been fulfilled. Odd that this was also the spot where so many Romans had thrown coins and that thousands of years earlier even prehistoric hunter-gatherers had felt the impulse to throw worked flints into the river here.

Returning now to the bridge or pier at Vauxhall, which jutted out from Thorney Island, it can hardly be a coincidence that this structure apparently led to one of the most important ritual sites in early London. We have seen that Thorney Island was a very important place in London's prehistory and perhaps the time has come to consider just why this patch of land was so sacred and why it later came to be the place from where, thousands of years later, the entire country is governed.

In the last chapter, we examined the idea of liminality – regions or zones where one thing changes into another. We saw that these zones can exist in both time and space. Some places have multiple liminal zones and the effect of this in the past was to make these areas particularly holy. In the case of Thorney Island, at least four or five liminal zones overlap. The most obvious of these liminalities are the fens and rivers which surround the island. Bogs were special places under any circumstances, as were islands. In the middle of the Thames, opposite Thorney Island, was a small island. So small was this gravel island that its liminal zone, the area adjacent to its shore, could be said to extend across the whole of the island. Another liminality which is to be found in the vicinity of Thorney Island is slightly less obvious.

Every river had its own character. Some were dedicated to or thought to be the homes of various deities and spirits. The region where one river met or flowed into another was thought to be special. At the modern-day district of Brentford in West London, for instance, the River Brent flows into the Thames just upstream from

Kew. The River Brent was at one time called the Bregant, which is without doubt a corruption of Brigantia, a British goddess. Brentford is really Brigantia's ford. The spot where the Bregant flowed into the Thames has provided a large number of votive offerings. The earliest of these date from the Stone Age, while others are extraordinary examples of Celtic metalwork. Brentford was also, as the very name implies, a ford. These two types of limanality, a ford and a confluence of two rivers combine at Brentford to create a specially place. This is illustrated in *figure 7.*

It has been suggested that it was at Brentford that Julius Caesar crossed the Thames during his second expedition to Britain in 54 BC, but this seems unlikely. The story arose because Caesar writes of the Britons planting sharpened stakes in the opposite bank to defend the crossing against the Roman troops. In fact, wooden stakes were found at Brentford some years ago, but there is no reason at all to suppose that they had been there for 2000 years. There would have been no reason at all for Caesar and his men to travel as far upstream as Brentford when a well-used ford was to be found near Thorney Island.

The section of the Thames at Thorney Island is significant for the fact that more than one river enters the Thames here: the several branches of the Tyburn which formed Thorney Island itself and also from the opposite bank, the Effra. The effect of these rivers flowing into the Thames from opposite directions was twofold. The religious effect was to multiply the holiness of this stretch of the river. The physical effect was to push up a small island in the middle of the Thames; an island so small, that it can be thought of as consisting entirely of liminal zone.

I have so far referred to Thorney Island in the singular. The reality was that, due to the nature of a river delta like that of the Tyburn at this time,

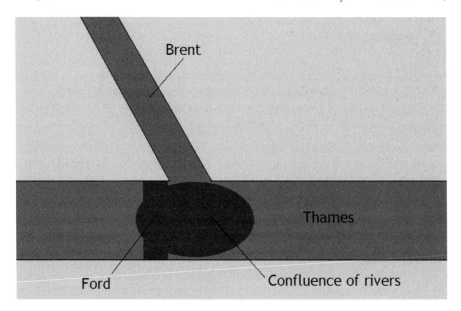

7 Overlapping zones of sacredness; the confluence of the Thames and the Brent

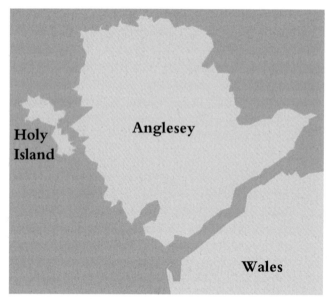

8 Anglesey and Holy Island

Thorney Island would most likely have consisted of at least two islands, one very much smaller than the other. We cannot at this late date know into how many branches the Tyburn divided when it reached the Thames. There is some evidence, though, to suppose that the island upon which Westminster Abbey was later built and the royal palace was placed was very small, no more than 30 acres or so.

There is an intriguing parallel with Thorney Island elsewhere in the British Isles. Oddly enough, it is to be found at the former 'headquarters' of the Druids on the island of Anglesey, off the coast of North Wales. *Figure 8* shows a rough sketch of this location. Many valuable items have been fished out of the lake called Llyn Cerrig Bach on Anglesey; it was used in the same way as Flag Fen and the Thames. It will be observed that in addition to the main island, close enough to the coast that the liminal zones of island and mainland overlap, there is a smaller island on the north-west tip of Anglesey. This is Holy Island and it is covered with prehistoric monuments.

Holy Island is not called so because of any sort of Christian association. Whatever the holiness here, it is to do with the aboriginal religion of Britain. Whether this too is some aspect of liminal zones, the juxtaposition of a larger and a smaller island together in this way seemed to magnify their sacred quality and the focus of this holiness or apartness seemed to be the smaller of the islands. There is another case of this happening in the British Isles. The holy island of Iona is also a small island next to a larger one – the Isle of Mull.

Looking again at London, we see that if the Menai Strait separating Anglesey from the Welsh mainland was narrow enough to smear the liminal zone out on to both island and mainland, how much more so would this have been the case with Thorney Island? Not only were the streams of the Tyburn narrow, but they separated Thorney not from dry land but from fenland; Bulinga Fen, in fact. We have already seen that fens in themselves were of importance, being almost all liminal zone, neither dry land nor water.

There are two more ways in which Thorney Island was important from a religious sense. This was the first point at which the Thames could be forded. In 1952 Baron Noel-Buxton forded the River Humber; allegedly the first time that this feat had been achieved since the Roman occupation. That summer, he attempted to prove that at low tide the Thames could still be forded at Westminster. He very nearly made it, needing only to swim for a few yards in the very middle of the river. The presence of a ford leading from the south bank of the Thames to Thorney Island was another demonstration of the special nature of this area. Fords are respected in many cultures as being of spiritual importance, mainly due to their liminal nature. When fording a river, is one on land or in the water? Both really.

Rivers like the Thames, with wide and extensive estuaries, are essentially a mixture of fresh and salt water for much of their length. Before embankments and bridges were built, the tidal head of the River Thames was at Westminster. It was at this point that an ocean-going ship could be carried upstream on the tide. More to the point, this was the region where fresh water became brackish or salty. Here is a very strange zone: where the salt sea meets the freshwater river.

In *figure 9* we can see a schematic representation of Thorney Island in the years before the Roman invasion and occupation. The zones of liminality have been marked and it will readily be seen that the whole island is engulfed in ritually important meaning: the ford, the bogs, the islands, the tributary rivers flowing into the great river and the meeting of salt and freshwater. It is hardly to be wondered at that this strange region was invested with power and went on to become the most important place in the whole country. In the next chapter we shall see how Thorney Island changed from being a cult centre and became instead the focus for political power in the city and also the entire country.

The overall consequence of all the various factors at which we have so far looked – ford, bridge, islands, fens and so on – was to make the area of modern-day Westminster enormously significant for those who once lived in the Thames valley. It was the nexus; the focal point where many aspects of the sacred came to a point. In 2010, an incredible discovery was made by archaeologists working right in front of MI6's headquarters at Vauxhall. This discovery underlines the importance of this stretch of the Thames to those living here thousands of years ago.

Six heavy wooden posts were found driven into the foreshore of the Thames. They were not in a straight line, nor were they arranged in a circle like the so-called Seahenge in Norfolk. Because they were only a few hundred yards from the Bronze Age bridge, which was found in 1993, it was at first assumed that these posts would be of roughly the same period, about 1500 BC. Incredibly, carbon dating showed them to date from 4500 BC, 3000 years older than the Vauxhall find. Beyond the obvious fact that they were part of a permanent structure, nobody has the least idea what these posts were doing by the river. They were placed there a thousand years before farming began in this country, at a time when the population moved from place to place in search of game and wild plants. The only huts which have been found from this period are flimsy shelters, meant only for temporary occupation.

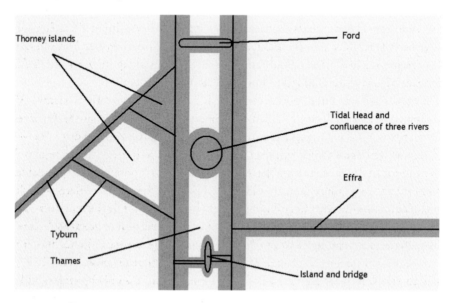

9a Zones of liminality around Thorney Island

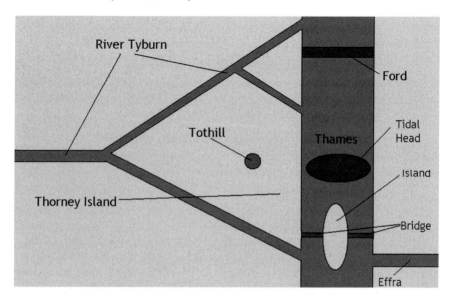

9b Schematic map of Thorney Island

It is a reasonable assumption that these 6500-year-old posts are part of ritual structure, rather than a house. Perhaps they were like totem poles or possibly they formed part of a platform built to enable the throwing of offerings into the river. Their discovery suggests that ritual practices in this area, close to Westminster, were well established almost 5000 years before the Roman invasion in AD 43.

Thorney Island was important, but it was not the only ritual centre in the Greater London area. We are never likely to know the full extent of the ritual landscape which lies beneath central London. Unlike the Roman walls and artefacts which come to light from time to time, most of the earlier religious structures were made of earth and wood; they have long been buried beneath the buildings and streets of modern London. We must move along the Thames a little to see what the ritual landscape of London itself was like.

South of, and in some cases under, Heathrow airport is a perfect example of the sort of ritual landscape which once stretched all the way along the Thames, covering most of London. Interlaced with the river were a number of earth-works which taken together give a very neat example of the various types of monuments which went into the making of a ritual landscape. They include a causewayed enclosure, henge and cursus. Close to them was a village which included a temple. Examining this perfect little cameo of a ritual landscape in the London area might give us some insight into the beliefs which motivated those living here 5000 years ago and caused them to rearrange the earth in this way for reasons wholly unconnected with shelter, food production, defence or survival. It will also show us what central London once looked like. It is only by understanding what these people thought was worth investing so much of their energy in that we shall be able to work out what life and death meant to them.

We begin with a site which is now lost to us forever. It was destroyed during gravel-digging operations in the early sixties and now lies beneath junction 13 of the M25 motorway. Around 3000 BC the people living near to the Thames at this point decided to construct a causewayed enclosure. Causewayed enclosures are found scattered across southern England. They consist of circular ditches which are interrupted by bridges or causeways leading into the central area. An illustration will make things clearer: *figure 10* shows a typical causewayed enclosure. The earth dug from the ditches was banked up around the perimeter of the enclosure. The one at Yeoveney Lodge, near Staines, which was excavated in the early 1960s, was about 160 yards across.

Nobody can say for sure what these enclosures were used for. They were not at all like hill forts; people did not live here nor were they defensible. Human remains are sometimes found and here might give a clue as to one of their uses. It is not uncommon to find skulls purposely buried in the ditches around the enclosure. Sometimes, burials have been carried out in the centre. There is also a lot of rubbish: remains of feasts, old broken pots, animal bones; all sorts of junk. This detritus has caused some archaeologists to suppose that causewayed

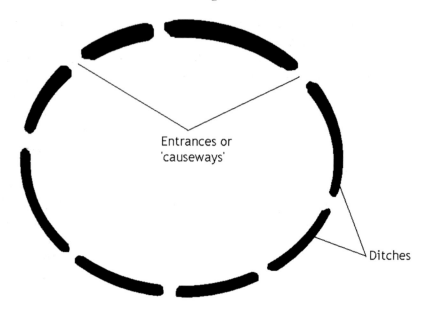

Entrances or 'causeways'

Ditches

10 Causewayed enclosure of the type found at Yeoveny Lodge

enclosures were used like fairgrounds or communal meeting places. Most likely, they were used for different things at different times. The presence of skulls, usually without their jawbones, hints that the Celtic preoccupation with severed heads may not have been peculiar to that culture, but might have its origins in the deeper past.

Mixed in with all the rubbish which seems to have been buried in pits or swept into the ditches of causewayed enclosures like that at Yeoveney Lodge are often human bones.

There is a bit of mystery about the number of skulls which have always turned up in prehistoric sites not only in London but also in the rest of Britain. It is often only skulls. They are found in wells, buried in ditches, thrown in rivers and concealed in the most unlikely places. What actually happened to human corpses during the Neolithic and Bronze Ages? We have plenty of skulls and complete skeletons in barrows, but where have all the other bones gone? The answer is not very pretty.

Wall paintings at Catal Huyuk in Turkey, one of the earliest towns in the world, show headless figures and vultures. It seems likely that the inhabitants there practised what is known as excarnation. This entails removing or allowing to be removed all the flesh from a human corpse. As a matter of fact, this method of dealing with corpses is still in use today around Bombay. It is used by the Parsees. This obscure religion, whose roots are in Iran, put corpses into so-called 'Towers of Silence'. They are exposed to the elements and vultures and crows then pick the flesh from them. Insects also go to work and, after a while, one is left with a sun-bleached and clean skeleton.

The human remains found within the long barrows, which were communal burial mounds, of the early Neolithic show distinct signs of excarnation. For one thing, there is no trace of decayed flesh, skin or hair or other organic matter where the bones are found. Had the flesh been removed by being scraped off by flint knives, there would be butchery marks on the bones; there are none. Another feature is that the skeletons are typically disarticulated; in lay terms, they have been pulled apart into bundles of bones before being placed into the barrows. The bones are also discoloured in a way which suggests that they have been exposed to the elements for some time before being placed in their final resting places. If we are guided by the evidence from Catal Huyuk and other places, it seems to be a fair guess that the method of excarnation used entailed exposing the bones to predators. It would have been no use just leaving them in a forest because wolves, bears and foxes would have done a little more than simply remove the flesh! These animals would have made off with the bones too.

The current thinking is that corpses were kept for a time in mortuary enclosures, placed on elevated wooden platforms perhaps, where birds like the carrion crow could have flocked to pull the soft tissues from them. Some purpose-built enclosures have definitely been identified, but it is thought that causewayed enclosures too may have been used for this purpose.

One hypothesis is that from very early times, the head and flesh were regarded as the important components of a human corpse. Once these were removed, the bones that were left over were just an inconvenient bundle to be dealt with as seemed best. Sometimes they were stacked up in long barrows, on other occasions just thrown into a ditch. Once there, most would have been removed by scavengers, being cracked open, chewed and splintered until they were unrecognisable.

A noticeable feature of the causewayed enclosure at Staines is that it was built on a gravel spit which actually jutted out into the Thames. The islands and promontories in London were also made of gravel covered in brick earth. Although none have yet been excavated, it would be surprising if similar enclosures were not a part of the landscape in central London; there was no shortage of gravel spits and islets in central London. The enclosure at Yeoveny Lodge was still in use during the Roman period. A polygonal structure was found during the investigations of the site and it seems that this spot continued to be of religious importance up to and including the Saxon invasions which followed the fall of the Roman Empire. This might explain why no traces of any causewayed enclosure like this have been uncovered in London itself. Such a site might be buried beneath a cathedral or church. The one at Yeoveny became the site of a Romano-Celtic shrine and it is quite likely that the same would have happened to any enclosure in London. It is by no means impossible that Southwark Cathedral, say, was built over a Neolithic structure of this kind.

Shepperton is more famous for its film studios than for its prehistoric remains. The town is near the Thames, a little to the south of Heathrow airport. In 1989, a circular henge was found nearby. This is a ditch and bank enclosure, in this case about 60ft in diameter. The bodies of two people were buried there, including a woman whose skeleton was the oldest ever unearthed in the Greater London area. Also buried there were deer skulls and dogs' skeletons – recurring motifs in religious sites in this country. This henge had its heyday about 5000 years ago and remained in use for over a thousand years. It was obviously a very important place for the inhabitants of this part of the Thames valley. Of great interest is the fact that the entrance to the enclosure pointed directly to the place where the sun rises on midsummer's day.

Henges were usually built near rivers and streams. The Shepperton henge was used for feasting, as the hearths and remains of cooked food show. It is likely that these meals may have been shared with the ancestors as often uneaten food is buried in ritual shafts at such places. A double row of wooden pillars or posts led from the entrance to Shepperton henge to the nearby river. We think of posts and poles now in strictly functional terms, as objects to mark a boundary or hold up a fence, but these wooden posts would most probably have been something quite different. What would this ceremonial path to the river have looked like when it was built? There are clues to be found in Greek and Roman writers of that time. Describing an open-air temple in Europe, Lucan, writing in the middle of the first century AD, says in his poem 'Pharsalia':

> *A grove there was, untouched by men's hands from ancient times, whose*
> *interlacing boughs enclosed a space of darkness and cold shade and*
> *banished the sunlight far above…water fell there in abundance from*
> *dark springs. The images of the gods, grim and rude, were uncouth*
> *blocks formed of felled tree trunks.*

These 'felled tree trunks' sound rather like native American totem poles. We can perhaps imagine tall posts, something like telegraph poles, carved in the likeness of gods and goddesses. Wooden images of gods like this have been found both near the Thames and at the source of the River Seine in France.

We are able at least to make intelligent guesses about henges and causewayed enclosures. About another part of the ritual landscape of West London, the Stanwell cursus, even guesswork is tricky and uncertain. Cursuses are only known in Britain and Ireland. They typically consist of two parallel ditches, the material from which is banked up between the ditches. The usual form is that this creates two ridges with a clear path between them. We have absolutely no idea what the purpose of these structures might have been. When first they were discovered, it was hypothesised that they might have been running tracks for ceremonial races. Some of them end at burial mounds and another possible purpose was that they allowed the spirits of the dead to move privately across the landscape.

The cursus, which passes beneath Heathrow airport, built almost 5000 years ago, is unusual in that its central pathway was raised, instead of being concealed as was more common. Usually, the earth from the twin ditches would be heaped into two separate banks, with a space between them for a path. This meant that anybody, living or dead, using this route would be invisible from outside the cursus. In the case of the Stanwell cursus, though, the ditches are so close together that the earth forms one solid bank. This means that the path between the ditches is on top of the earth and that anybody walking along this cursus would be visible from miles away.

Associated with the Stanwell cursus are some postholes which were in place before its construction. They are similar to the postholes found at the Shepperton henge and also at other ancient ritual sites such as Stonehenge. All we know for certain is that tall posts or poles were erected across the landscape for come ceremonial reason. In Chapter 8, I suggest a possible explanation for the cursuses.

The first religious practices in the capital about which we know anything definite are those of the Celts. What we know is second or third hand, from classical authors who themselves learned about the subject from returning soldiers and administrators; but it is better than nothing. Often, these accounts tie in with archaeological finds, which provide some confirmation of what has been described by writers such as Strabo and Julius Caesar. One thing about which we can be confident is that the religious meetings of the ancient Britons took place not in buildings but in the open air. This is in sharp contrast to present-day religious practice in this country, where organised worship almost invariably takes place inside specially constructed buildings. This idea, that religious observance must be associated with a clearly delineated space or enclosure was started in Britain by the Romans.

In prehistoric London, certain areas were believed to be sacred and particularly suited to contact with the gods or the spirits of the dead. River banks and hilltops were especially favoured places. There was something essentially vague and indeterminate about the extent of these natural locations. One could not take another step and suddenly find oneself outside the holy ground. No physical, man-made structure was needed for worship or sacrifice; it was the very earth, water and trees which were seen to be important. Where a spring bubbled up from the underworld, the surrounding area was of course holy, but it would be absurd to set a boundary on this holiness and say that it stopped precisely 20ft from the water's edge. Holiness and sanctity are not really like that. Like a bright source of light, they diffuse outward and there is no point at which one can say, 'This is where the illumination ends; right here'. Rather, the effects of the radiance fade away, growing fainter and fainter, until they can no longer be seen.

For the Romans, this was not altogether satisfactory. They wished to mark out the limits of temples and holy places clearly; a possible consequence of living in towns and cities, although they even tended to do this when a temple was set in the middle of open ground, miles from the nearest house. It was as though they felt uncomfortable with the idea of uncontained sacredness and felt the need to contain it within a special enclosure. This is a move away from the concept of a ritual landscape in which the whole of the land was part of the religious backdrop, towards the modern way of limiting religion to a few isolated and self-contained pockets within an irreligious context. *Colour plate 7* shows a reconstruction of the Romano-Celtic temple at Greenwich. This is a fairly typical temple of the time and makes the situation which we are discussing a little clearer.

The temple itself is the colonnaded building on the left. Surrounding the complex is a wall. This marks the limits of the temenos or sacred enclosure. Prayers might be offered in the temple by a priest or a sacrifice carried out, but the laity would advance no further than the courtyard enclosed by the temenos wall. This was in keeping with Roman customs of religion and quite different from the way that things had been done in this country up until AD 43. It is quite plain that at Greenwich, one was on holy ground inside the temenos, but by stepping out through the gate, one was back at once in the secular world.

A perfect instance of this process and the Roman view of the matter can be seen at Bath. Before the Romans came, the hot spring at Bath was the centre point of an eldritch landscape whose appearance must have been awe-inspiring: dark green pools, rimmed with orange deposits of iron; the whole area wreathed in clouds of vapour. This was the abode of a goddess called Sulis and her influence stretched out across the countryside. Pilgrims came here to pay their respects and leave her gifts.

The Romans were quite prepared to accept Sulis as being cognate with their own goddess Minerva, but they were not at all keen on the slovenly, haphazard conditions to be seen at her place of worship. They built masonry walls round the pool, channelled the spring through lead pipes and put up a proper temple in the classical style with a triangular pediment. By the time that they had finished, the whole effect was very civilised and neat; there was none of the untrammelled nature that the Britons had been content to endure. The sacredness had been contained and defined.

We still have the arrangements of the Romano-Celtic temple complexes in our churches and graveyards. Often a church will be sited within a walled area where the dead are buried and the whole area around the church is seen as being sacred. This is consecrated ground, specially blessed by a priest. The parallel with the Romano-Celtic temple and its surrounding temenos is exact.

This process of restricting religion to special places and times had already begun before the Roman invasion. Even before the invasion, the religious contract was weakening, being observed more as form than from inner conviction. At the same time, religion was splitting off from everyday life, beginning the process which would ultimately end in today's secular society. The arrival of the Romans, with their more 'sophisticated' form of religion may well have acted as a catalyst, accelerating this division, but it did not cause it.

One example should make it clear how religious practices had changed in London by the end of the Roman occupation. In the years before the arrival of the Romans, many votive offerings were made to the rivers of London. These began with flint axes and culminated with the sacrifice of exquisitely made bronze helmets and shields. These were articles which made a statement about the owner. He was prosperous and yet prepared to dispose of his wealth by giving it freely to his ancestors or the god of the river. Let us fast forward a couple of centuries and see how votive offerings were being made around AD 200.

The first thing we notice is that the value of the offerings has declined drastically. Nobody is now casting elaborate pieces of armour into the river. Nor are swords found from this period. Instead, we find small, cheap items. Instead of swords and shields, there are knives. The other very noticeable thing is that many of these things are worn out or broken. Rather than sacrificing a brand new sword, those making votive offerings are instead giving to the gods various bits of junk for which they have no further use. It is rare to find worn out or broken tools and weapons from the Bronze Age – those which were given as votive offerings are almost without exception in perfect condition. This makes the contrast with the later offerings from the Roman period especially stark. These later citizens of London were like us. Religion was just one part of their life. Instead of a ritual landscape, we have a 'temple district'. Religion is being squeezed into a special area. The same thing happened with the enclosures around the Romano-Celtic temples of this period; the sacred had limits set upon it, whereas before it had encompassed the entire land. The process of compressing religion into smaller and smaller, well-defined locations has continued up to the present day.

London has always been a religious centre. It began as an entire landscape, where every hill and river was sacred in some way. Slowly, over thousands of years, the situation changed and the holiness became focused in a few special places. Even these shrank, until the sacred ground was walled off and eventually became only a single building here and there.

This physical limitation of the sacred was mirrored by a corresponding temporal contraction. During the Neolithic and Bronze Age, the grand age of monument building and shaping of the ritual landscape, all activity was in a sense religious. This applied alike to the flint miner and those knapping axe heads, the bridge builder and the men hauling stones across country to build a passage tomb. There was no demarcation between work and leisure, secular and divine. By the beginning of the Iron Age in this country, around 800 BC, this was changing. Wooden shrines were being built, perhaps to localise religion and limit its observance. We saw a temple of this kind at Caesar's Camp.

This compartmentalisation of religion increased with the arrival of the Romans. Religion became something one did, rather than an integral part of ordinary life. Just as certain places became devoted to religion, so too did special times: ceremonies at different times of the year, sacrifices before a journey or as a thanksgiving for the birth of a child. Since the Romans left, this same process has continued unabated. During the Middle Ages, church attendance was a regular obligation; a part of one's time which was dedicated to God. By the nineteenth century this had become for most a weekly ritual, limited to Sundays and special festivals. In our own time, the time spent on religion for many people has dwindled away almost to nothing. The churches are full at Christmas, but apart from that, most of us only use them for marriages and baptisms. The religious landscape has shrunk to a handful of special buildings and a few hours each year spent in them.

Of course, the religion of the Celts in Britain did not spring from nowhere. It was based in part upon the myths and beliefs of the Bronze Age farmers whom they supplanted. This in turn was founded upon the ideas of the Neolithic and before that the Palaeolithic hunter-gatherers, who lived here for hundreds of thousands of years before the start of agriculture and a settled lifestyle. This explains the enduring image of the hunter and stag and their hybrid form, the horned god. Stags were enormously important to the earliest inhabitants of this country and so was hunting.

Other parallels from cultures with no apparent link to Europe are to be seen in the special reverence and awe accorded to horned animals, such as bulls. From both the golden calf of the Israelites and one of the first towns of which we have knowledge, Catal Huyuk on the Anatolian plateau of Turkey, we are able to see the cult of the horned beast.

There was a widespread bull cult throughout the Middle East in Biblical times. The Israelites' idea of creating a golden idol in the form of a young bull did not occur in a vacuum. From Egypt to Assyria, the bull was the ultimate expression of power, ferocity and virility. Gods and bulls went hand in hand. Sometimes the gods rode on their backs, on other occasions they slew bulls as a demonstration of their mastery of nature. In Europe, the outward attributes of the stag were grafted on to humans. Antlers sprouting from the head of a man are shown in a number of carvings and paintings from prehistoric Europe. In the cultures of the Middle East, human and bovine characteristics were similarly combined, but in a more obvious and less human fashion. The horned figures from Britain and the continent are, apart from the antlers or horns on their heads, plainly human. In the eastern Mediterranean and further, the hybrid creatures were definitely not human: the fearsome minotaur, for instance – a man with a bull's head – or the winged bulls of Assyria, with human heads. The human-headed bulls featured too in the temple at Jerusalem, as did bronze bulls as cult animals in the forecourt. This is a similar image to the Western European tradition, but with clear differences.

The bones of oxen are found at ritual sites in this country too, notably at Shepperton. There is no doubt that horned and antlered animals had a special significance for the people who lived here thousands of years ago. In Chapter 5 we will look in detail at the gods and goddesses of Britain, but before doing so we must look a little more closely at the cult centre which grew up around Westminster.

4

A Tale of Two Cities

The story of London is the story not of one city, but two. We are so used to this concept that we hardly even notice it. When a commentator on the television news refers to the view in the 'City', we automatically translate this as being concerned solely with financial or business matters. If, on the other hand, somebody talks of opinion in 'Westminster', we know at once that the topic is politics and the governance of the country. This is unambiguous and our view of London is rooted in this sharp division between commerce and government, the City and Westminster. They are two separate and distinct entities.

For at least a thousand years, the Royal family of this country have refused to live in their capital city itself. Instead, they have insisted in setting up their palaces and national religious centre a few miles from the City of London on Thorney Island. This is a pretty strange situation and it is worth looking at how it came to be this way. After all, it would be far more logical for the monarch to have lived within the walled city of his capital, rather than making his home beyond the city walls in an area of marshland. Even today, the queen lives in a palace which is built quite literally on top of the River Tyburn, on the very edge of Thorney Island. This is, of course, part of London now, but when this custom began, Westminster was nowhere near the City of London.

The City of London, the so-called Square Mile, is the financial and business heart of the country. The Bank of England, the Stock Exchange, all the big businesses and so on are to be found in the City of London itself. This is roughly the area of Roman Londinium – the part of central London that was walled round. That this district should be the commercial centre of London makes a lot of sense. London was originally founded not as a political centre but a trading port. The Square Mile simply maintains this tradition.

What is odd and needs a little explaining is how it came to be that the political and religious power in the London area came to rest not in the walled city, but a couple of miles away in Westminster. This dichotomy is enshrined in law and tradition. When the queen approaches the City of London, her procession halts at Temple Bar, the point where the City of Westminster becomes the City of London. She waits there until the Lord Mayor of London invites her into the City of London by offering his sword. More than this, it is also the custom that the Lord Mayor's party should be dressed as elaborately as the courtiers of a medieval monarch, whereas those in the royal procession are dressed more soberly. There is no doubt in the minds of those watching these ceremonies that the queen is being granted permission to enter and that, in the City itself, she is a visitor and a guest.

This is an extraordinary state of affairs. The monarch of the entire realm is asking permission to visit the heart of her own capital city! What could possibly have happened in the past to give rise to such a situation? To see how this came about, it is necessary to go back 2000 years to the Roman invasion.

The first Roman capital of this country was not London but Colchester. There was already a flourishing city there, Camulodunum, and there was sea access as well. For the first few years of the occupation, the centre of power in Roman-occupied Britain was definitely at Colchester rather than London. Just why this changed a few years after the Boudican revolt has been a bit of a puzzle. It almost seems that after the destruction of Colchester, Londinium and Verulamium in AD 60, the Romans made a conscious decision to adopt London as their main base rather than Colchester. This might indeed be exactly what happened. To understand why, we must think a little about the Roman attitude to the religious beliefs of those whom they conquered. Almost without exception, the Romans were exceedingly tolerant and open minded about the gods worshipped in the countries of their empire. Sometimes, they adopted those gods for their own, as happened in Mithraism, a Persian religion which became very popular in the Roman army. There was also in London a temple of Isis, who was of course an Egyptian goddess. In Britain, the gods of Rome and the native British gods often became joined together; Mars-Camulus and Apollo-Cunomaglos, for instance. The Romans were happy to allow other gods and religions to operate alongside their own religious system.

There were, in the history of the Roman Empire, only two cases where the indigenous religious practices were actively suppressed. Israel was one such country and Britain was the other. It is fairly easy to see why Rome should lose patience with the Jewish leaders in Israel. The whole society in that country was heavily influenced by the dictates of their religion. This told the citizen what work could be done and when, the food which could be eaten, decoration in the home, clothing, financial matters; all these and more were properly the business of the Sadducees of the temple and the lay preachers known as Pharisees.

The rulings of their religious leaders brought the ordinary Jews into conflict with the occupying army. It was like having two governments, the civil Roman administration and the religious administration in Jerusalem. It was hardly to be wondered at that the tensions engendered by such a situation should eventually have spilled over into open rebellion, which came six years after the Boudican revolt in Britain. The Romans blamed the Jewish leadership for this war. It is likely that the same thing happened in this country; that is to say that the religious leaders encouraged the people to rebel against the occupying forces. Druidism had, after all, been bloodily suppressed in Gaul and the Druids here might have thought that this could be payback time.

The influence of religion in Britain during the first century AD was at least as extensive as it was in Israel. We know that there was little division between religious and civil life. The leaders of religion at that time were, of course, the Druids and their position was a powerful one. There were three main classes in British society: warriors, Druids and farmers. The warrior class included the nobility and held the political power. They were, however, dependent upon the Druids. The Druids were not restricted to any particular region or tribe. A Druid of the Catuvellauni had as much respect if he visited the Atrebates as one of their own Druids. The Druids could, in effect, excommunicate anybody and cut them off from the religious life of the people. Since religion and everyday life were hardly separate, this was a heavy penalty. They also acted as judges and lawgivers, whom even the kings were forced to acknowledge. They were the intermediaries between man and the gods, and whoever offended against the Druids offended against the gods themselves.

All this meant that British society at that time was effectively a theocracy, a type of society which is all but unknown in the world today. The closest modern comparison is probably a country like Iran, where the religious leaders ultimately have more real power than those who are ostensibly in charge. It took the Romans a decade or so after the Claudian invasion of AD 43 to grasp fully the situation and when they did, they acted decisively. The very fact that religious life, industry and civil society in general should be so inextricably entwined made the pacification of this country all but impossible without cutting away the leaders of the religion: the Druids.

There was another reason why the Romans decided finally to suppress the Druids and that was their penchant for human sacrifice. It might seem strange that the Romans, not notably a squeamish nation or over-concerned about shedding blood themselves, should disapprove so strongly of the occasional human sacrifice; but they regarded the practice as being barbarous. This meant that, in addition to the pragmatic decision to put an end to what was, in effect, a parallel government, the Romans were motivated also by a principled opposition to what they saw as a disgusting and reprehensible custom.

The main sanctuary of the Druids was the island of Anglesey, which lies off the coast of North Wales. In AD 59/60 a military force under the command of Seutonius Paulus launched an amphibious assault on this stronghold. Every single Druid found there, male and female, was put to the sword or thrown alive into funeral pyres. Even by the standards of Rome, this was an especially brutal action and it almost certainly helped to precipitate Boudica's revolt a few months later. Tacitus described the destruction of this stronghold:

> On the coastline, a line of warriors of the opposition was stationed, mainly made up of armed men, amongst them women, with their hair blowing in the wind, while they were carrying torches. Druids were amongst them, shouting terrifying spells, their hands raised towards the heavens, which scared our soldiers so much that their limbs became paralysed. As a result, they remained stationary and were injured. At the end of the battle, the Romans were victorious, and the holy oaks of the Druids were destroyed.

This is, incidentally, a hint that the society in Britain at that time leaned towards the matriarchal. The Romans were disgusted at the freedom shown by the women of Britain, as evidenced by their attitude towards Boudica. That even at the main base of the Druids was to be found women suggests a degree of equality unusual in the classical world. Here again, though, might be an example of an order or tradition lingering on in this country. At both Lepenski Vir and Catal Huyuk, it seems likely that women did at least as much as the men. Indeed, it is possible that it was women who did the bulk of the farming and at least some of the hunting. If, as has been hypothesised here, Britain retained some of the beliefs and practices of the Palaeolithic long after they had vanished from mainland Europe, then it is quite possible that in addition to retaining religious ideas which had been abandoned in most of mainland European, the people on these islands also held on to a wholly different set of ideas about the appropriate roles of men and women. No Roman woman could have ruled the country or led an army in the way that Boudica did, nor can one readily imagine Roman women fighting side by side with the soldiers as they did at Anglesey when defending it against attack by a foreign army.

It is no coincidence that the headquarters of the Druids, the religious leaders of Britain, should have been on an island. We have seen the mystical importance of such places with their surrounding zone of liminality. Anglesey may have been the main religious centre in Britain, but there were without doubt regional centres as well. One of these was probably Thorney Island. There are a number of reasons for supposing this to be so.

When the Romans came to Britain for good in AD 43, a century after the first, tentative expedition by Julius Caesar, they crossed the River Thames at London. Cassius Dio, writing over a century later, mentions two intriguing snippets of information about what became known as the Claudian invasion in AD 43. For one thing, he says that when the Romans reached the Thames, they crossed the river by means of a bridge (pontem). He gives no further details and we cannot be sure whether he is referring to a pre-existing structure built by the Britons or some sort of pontoon erected by Roman engineers. Cassius Dio then relates that the Roman forces marched on the city of Camulodunum or Colchester, as it later became known. The accounts of the campaign make definite and unambiguous mention of a road or 'via' leading from the Thames to Colchester. This is quite astonishing. Such a road would have been 50 miles long and running through thick forest for much of the way. Such a civil engineering operation would have required a huge amount of manpower for a considerable length of time. What would its purpose have been?

There was, after all, no city or large settlement at London. All the evidence suggests that the only thing to be found in London was a religious sanctuary surrounded by barrows and shrines. Was this the reason for constructing this road as a route for pilgrims? One thing is certain: the tribes living in Essex at that time would not go to all this trouble just for the convenience of a handful of travellers. A road, rather than a simple track, would have been used by horses, carts and chariots. There must have been a fair amount of traffic in order to make the thing worthwhile.

When the 'Sweet Track', named after the man who discovered it, Ray Sweet, came to light in Somerset in 1970, there was great excitement. This wooden trackway was built over 5000 years ago so that travellers could make their way across the swampy land of the Somerset Levels. Since then, other trackways of the same sort have turned up in various locations, not least in London. Now one can quite see why a track across the marshes and wetlands of Somerset might have been a useful project for the farmers of the district. The ones found in London are a little more puzzling. The standard picture of London before the Romans is that there was hardly anything or anybody here. True, occasional plough marks have been seen, but nothing to suggest that this was an inhabited area. It was hardly prime agricultural land, consisting as it did of swamps and marsh. Yet a system of wooden tracks had been set down from East London on both sides of the Thames, seemingly leading towards the city and Westminster. The most recent of these trackways to be examined, near to Belmarsh Prison in Woolwich, has been dated to 4000 BC, 500 years older than Stonehenge.

There is another clue which leads one to think that the London area was somehow sacred to many people. Londinium was first built on the triple hills beside the Thames in around AD 50. For the next 10 years, it was a port, military base and frontier town. The orthodox view is that this raw new town was occupied by soldiers, sailors, traders, builders and labourers. One could guess that it would be full in general of healthy young men. When Boudica and her army descended upon the city in AD 60, Seutonius, fresh from his victory in Anglesey, made the tactical decision to abandon Londinium to its fate. Those living there were under no illusions as to what their fate was likely to be when the Iceni army arrived.

Nevertheless, Tacitus relates that many of the inhabitants remained behind when the army evacuated the city. These were citizens who were unable to travel fast enough to keep up with the army columns by reason of their old age or sex. Intriguingly, there was another class who remained behind. These were those who were, according to Tacitus, 'attached to the place'. One has to wonder who all these people were. Where had the old people come from and what were they doing in London? Could traders who had been living in this rough outpost for only a few years really have become so attached to the place that they would rather stay, facing almost certain death, than flee to the forests? And where had all the women come from? Were these British people or Romans?

There is something more than a little strange about the attachment shown to this new town by so many of its citizens. One can hardly believe that a motley collection of Roman shopkeepers and their wives would be prepared to stay put and face the wrath of Boudica and her warriors because they had become so fond of this patch of the Thames valley. If, on the other hand, we assume that many of those living in the city were British people who had come to live in the liminal zone of the Thames because of ancient and traditional associations, this begins to make a little more sense. These would be men and women for whom London was something more than a Roman frontier post. It was a few miles from the holiest place they knew and living here was to them rather like a Catholic moving to within walking distance of the Vatican or a Muslim going to live near Mecca. If these analogies are anything near the mark, it makes the whole situation surrounding the military evacuation of Londinium a lot more comprehensible.

Whatever the motive for staying put in the city, religious or otherwise, Boudica and her army regarded all those whom they found in the Roman city as enemies. Either they were Romans or, worse, British collaborators. When she arrived, the city was sacked, everybody found there murdered in various disgusting ways and the buildings torched.

Until the Romans settled here after AD 43, the entire liminal zone along the Thames, including the area which would later become London was very sparsely inhabited. Those living here may have been hermits and ascetics. During the Iron Age it is likely that the Druids were in charge of worship and pilgrimage. This was a ritual landscape, with many monuments and shrines, but few people. The Roman invaders at once thought that this was an ideal spot for a port and urban centre. Why did they not stamp their authority immediately upon the region by seizing the sacred Thorney Island and using that for their base? There are two reasons.

When first they landed in Britain, the Romans could have had little idea just how powerful and all-pervasive were the religious feelings of the tribes who lived here. They had suppressed the Druids in Gaul, but Britain was a far more dedicated centre of the religion than France had ever been. Perhaps the Romans were unaware of this, although Caesar himself had written in *The Gallic Wars*: 'It is thought that the doctrine of the Druids was invented in Britain and was brought from there to Gaul; even today those who want to study the doctrine in greater detail usually go to Britain to learn there.'

We have seen how flexible in general the Romans were in religious questions and almost certainly their hope was to reach some sort of accommodation with the Druids, who were at that time the organised priesthood of the British. They greatly underestimated the influence of the Druids, though. Clearly, they believed that with a little give and take, their gods could rub along with our own and that there was no need to provoke a fight over this. So although they set upon this part of the Thames valley for their new town, they did not find it necessary or desirable to begin by clashing with the Britons by violating their sanctuary.

The other reason for establishing Londinium where they did was purely strategic. Thorney Island was a piece of boggy land surrounded by mudflats and marshes. A worse place for a military base would be hard to find. Even the streams were brackish and muddy. Ludgate, Cornhill and Tower Hill, though, were dry and provided defensible ground. They were supplied with bubbling streams of clear, fresh water. From a military perspective, they were more suitable for a base than the marshes.

After Boudica was defeated in the Midlands, Colchester was sidelined. London was not only rebuilt, but it became the most important city in Britain. Some idea of its significance can be seen when we learn that its basilica was the largest north of the Alps. From being a fairly small military camp, not on a par with the main city at Colchester, London suddenly grows in both size and importance after the Boudican revolt. Not only that, but buildings are erected and burials conducted on Thorney Island, a couple of miles outside the city walls.

This change of the centre of gravity of the province of Britannia from Colchester to London has puzzled some historians. The most likely explanation lies in the destruction of the Druids' headquarters at Anglesey. The Romans had realised that the Druids were more of a unifying influence for the British than they had bargained for and that, until Druidism was stamped out once and for all, there would always be the possibility of another rebellion. When Seutonius had defeated Boudica, it would be logical if the next step were to be the crushing of all other centres of Druidism in Britain. That a religious sanctuary had existed on Thorney Island for thousands of years seems indisputable. We have seen Christianity taking over religious sites and there is every reason to believe that the Druids would have done the same thing before the Christians. By increasing the size of London and making it the main city of the province, while simultaneously taking over Thorney Island, the Britons would receive a warning. Rome was the power now, both political and religious. Establishing a presence on Thorney Island would be hugely symbolic act. The native religion was not crushed or suppressed, but the priesthood had been driven out or killed and one of their sanctuaries and groves destroyed.

Figure 11 shows the position of Londinium and its relation to Thorney Island. It will readily be appreciated that there is a considerable distance between these two places. This made it all the more noticeable when Edward the Confessor left the walled City of London and had an abbey and palace built on Thorney Island.

The replacement of wooden shrines and groves with traditional square buildings of stone was a form of cultural imperialism. Not only the outward signs of

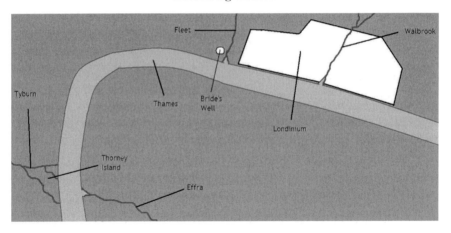

11 Londinium in relation to Thorney Island

religious observance were changed, but the British gods were to be reminded that they too were subsidiary to the gods of Rome. They were worshipped as Apollo-Cunomaglos, Mars-Alator and so on. The religion of Britain was now firmly linked to that of Rome.

Having cleansed Anglesey of Druidism, the Romans were hardly likely to have allowed it to flourish elsewhere in the province. Under Roman law, burials were not permitted within the walls of a city. In Londinium, they therefore established a graveyard just outside the city gate at Bishopsgate. There was probably another cemetery outside the Ludgate gate, across the River Fleet at the foot of modern-day Fleet Street. What reason could there have been for conducting funerals 2 miles away in the marshes of Thorney Island? The answer is fairly obvious. Just as the Christians in the first thousand years or so of the Christian era made a point of setting their churches and cathedrals upon pre-existing shrines and holy places, so too with the Romans. We have seen that the wooden shrines of the British and their sacred springs were built over in the Roman style. Thorney Island would have been a very important place upon which for Rome to stamp its identity. It had been a place of worship and sacrifice for thousands of years and was almost certainly supervised by the Druids at the time that Londinium was founded.

Just as with other religious sites, it would have made perfect sense for the Romans to erect a temple of their own at this important cult centre and dedicate it to a god of their own, in this case Apollo. Conducting funerals of their own there would have had the effect of emphasising to the natives that Thorney Island was no longer their own special and exclusive place.

William Camden, an Elizabethan antiquary, wrote:

> By this suburb Westminster, which some time was more than a mile distant, is
> conjoined so close unto the City of London that it seems a member thereof,
> whereas it is a City of it self, having their peculiar magistrates and privileges. It

was called in times past Thorney of Thornes, but now Westminster of the West situation and the Monastery. Most renowned it is for that Church, the Hall of Justice, and the Kings palace. This Church is famous especially by reason of the Inauguration and Sepulchar of the kings of England. Sulcard writes that there stood sometimes a Temple of Apollo in that place, and that in the days of Antonius Pius it fell down with an earthquake.

There are references too in the Welsh Chronicle of Tysilio. He tells how Bladud, father of King Lear, made a pair of wings and then flew with them. He ended up falling from the sky, right on top of the temple of Apollo in London which resulted in his death. Britain's first recorded aeronautical accident! There is little doubt that a Roman building did stand where Westminster Abbey is today and the chances are that it was indeed a temple of some sort. That it was dedicated to Apollo is not unlikely. In the last few years, more and more evidence has emerged of the Roman presence in this part of London. So much so that archaeologists now talk of 'Roman Westminster'. In 2006, a Roman coffin was found during building works at St Martin-in-the-Fields church at Trafalgar Square. Roman masonry was seen during other work many years ago. What better way for the occupying forces to show that this part of the country now belonged to them than to use it as a vast cemetery?

The Roman occupation, though, lasted only a few brief centuries. Set against the perspective of thousands of years of continuous use of a religious site, the Roman involvement would have been over in the blink of an eye. The next wave of settlers found much in London with which they were readily able to identify.

The Saxons and Vikings who succeeded the Romans shared many beliefs with the British. Their versions of the gods and mythic archetype were a lot closer to the British way of thought than were the more sophisticated avatars of their gods which had been imported by Rome. Diana and Mercury were pale and effete foreigners compared to the earthy gods and goddesses of the Germans, British and Norsemen.

We know that it did not take the Saxons long to fall into the old ways of Britain. The re-use of the Bronze Age cemetery in Greenwich tells us that. So too does the practice of making votive offerings into the Thames, which continued without a pause. For their part, those living in this country were also happy to welcome the Norse and Germanic gods. They were, after all, their own gods, albeit called by unfamiliar names. No wonder that we were happy to incorporate their gods and goddesses into the days of the week. Every Wednesday we still celebrate the enduring image of Woden, the one-eyed hunting god, leader of the Wild hunt.

The new settlers recognised the true nature of London from the very beginning. They tended to avoid the walled city of Londinium and gravitated instead along the Strand towards Thorney Island. The Roman city was ignored as irrelevant. Here was a complete city, lately abandoned and standing ready for occupation and yet it seemed to hold no attraction for the newcomers. They were drawn by some ancient impulse towards Thorney Island, although forbidden by ancient and deeply held taboos from actually living there. It retained its status as the pre-eminent religious site of the country. The Saxon city was called Lundenwic and it stretched along the north shore of the Thames, roughly midway between London and Westminster. Most archaeological finds from this period have been clustered around the Strand.

The Saxons, Angles and Jutes who flocked into the country in the centuries after the fall of Rome were not Christians. They shared the same belief system as those who were living here. When the Vikings arrive a few centuries later, they too followed what Christians would describe as 'pagan' gods. It was not for a further couple of centuries that Christianity became the 'official' religion of Britain. In the meantime, missionaries were arriving from the continent and there were conversions. These were sporadic and in general men and women were free to follow their own ways.

It was not until the middle of the ninth century that the City of London regained its position as the main area of habitation in this part of the Thames valley. Later on, after the battle of Hastings and the Norman invasion, the Normans knew a good thing when they saw it: a dry and habitable square mile of land with walls around it that could easily become a practically impregnable city. It was the Normans who built a great stone fortress there to reinforce and underline to the Saxons their ownership of this part of the country. However, a few years before they came here, something curious happened on Thorney Island.

The Christians had already built a church on Thorney Island in the seventh century. When Edward the Confessor came to the throne in 1044, he wished to reinforce the hold of Christianity upon the London area. Although nominally a Christian nation, the old religion was still very popular, particularly among the ordinary people. Thorney Island was still held in awe. Edward decided to build a huge abbey on Thorney, a Christian establishment which would once and for all eradicate any pagan allegiance to this inhospitable spot. Not only did he build his abbey, he had a palace built right next to it and moved the whole royal and political power of England away from London and to this obscure but greatly revered location.

From the time of Edward the Confessor, right up to the present day, Westminster has been the seat of government and the home of the royal family. Every monarch has been anointed and crowned there in the abbey which Edward caused to be built. The holiness which was associated with Thorney from the time of the Stone Age has transferred to the monarchy, the church and the political leadership of the country. In times of crisis, crowds gravitated as recently as the two world wars to congregate outside parliament or Buckingham Palace. The transformation is now complete and Thorney Island is the heart of all power in Britain, just as it was 3000 or 4000 years ago.

5

Gods and Goddesses

Something which modern western readers may find a little disconcerting is the extent to which the deities of the prehistoric world mutated and were in some sense interchangeable. Kings and chieftains became gods; gods declined and became human or sunk even further and became devils. In Chapter 6 we will see how the goddess Brigantia became the human saint, Bridget. The same thing happened to mighty Cernunnos, who degenerated into a man, Herne the Hunter. Of course for the Romans, the process also occurred in the opposite direction as their emperors attained the status of gods. It might also be observed that this happened in Christianity, where confusion arose as to whether the man Jesus became elevated to the status of a god or if God had become man.

Perhaps we should not be too surprised at the way that gods rise and fall in the course of time. We have become indoctrinated over the last 1500 years or so with the Christian notion of God as infallible, omnipotent and unchanging. For prehistoric men and women, the notion of omnipotence and timelessness had not yet emerged. For them, men, women and gods were much the same; rational entities that simply had different powers and sometimes shared the same physical world. Halfway between ordinary people and gods was the shaman or magician.

The shaman dwelt in two worlds: the world of men and the land of spirits and gods. He had more powers than most people and could influence events in mysterious ways. Once this is understood, we can see that it is not a great leap to viewing gods and goddesses as being a bit like invisible shamans or medicine men. They have many human traits such as greed, anger, vanity, foolishness and a tendency to fall in love with the wrong person. In short, the gods are pretty much like us, except that we can't see them and they have a few additional superhero powers. When we look at the image of the 'sorcerer' from the cave painting at Trois Frères, it is in a sense meaningless to ask ourselves whether this is a shaman or god; he is both.

One hundred and fifty years ago Ludwig Feuerbach wrote that 'God is man writ large'. It is only by reflecting upon the truth of this statement that we shall be able to understand how the first inhabitants of the London area saw their gods and goddesses. They were really just humans who had somehow been elevated a little in status. Just as sometimes a special person could attain divinity, so too could other gods slip back and become human beings again. This would have been a very familiar idea to the Romans and before them the Greeks. Their gods were passionate and full blooded, prone to making mistakes and doing the wrong thing. Only relatively recently have we become enamoured of a faultless god who can do no wrong nor make any error. Little wonder that we prefer to see the human face of this mighty and infallible god, worshipping in his place the avatar of the Galilean Jew Jesus, with his human personality, instead of the invisible and almighty God in Heaven who is so difficult to comprehend.

When the Romans came to this country, they found a pantheon of gods and goddesses being worshipped by the native inhabitants. These deities became, over the course of time, linked to the Roman gods. Camulos, the British god of war, became Mars-Camulos or Mars-Alator; the Lord of the Hounds, Cunomaglos, became an avatar of Apollo and was worshipped as Apollo-Cunomaglos. It is hard to believe that a Victorian missionary of the nineteenth century would be as tolerant of other gods. One cannot imagine an English clergyman in India accepting that Christ was just an avatar of Krishna and referring to Christ-Krishna! Perhaps this is because the god of the Jews and Christians is, as the Bible tells us, an exceedingly jealous god. The Bible is quite specific about this question. In the book of Exodus (Ex. 20:4–5), we read this attitude to other gods: 'You shall not worship them or serve them; for I, the LORD your God, *am a jealous God*'. This would have been utterly incomprehensible to any Roman or Celt of the first century AD.

When discussing the religious practices and beliefs of those who lived in the Thames valley thousands of years ago, we face a very tricky problem. Those early Britons had no written language. We must therefore rely upon either scanty archaeological evidence or the writings of classical authors such as Julius Caesar or Strabo. Archaeological evidence may be ambiguous and what a Roman military commander has to say about the customs of a defeated nation may not be altogether objective. They had, after all, a vested interest in portraying the nations whom they had vanquished as being brutal and debased, likely to benefit from the enlightened ways of those who were bringing them the advantages of civilised society. It will be remembered that this was the same line taken by the British a few millennia later, when they were imposing their own ways upon so-called barbarians. Bearing all this in mind, what can we say about the gods and goddesses which were worshipped at sites in London before the Roman occupation?

One thing which we can state with confidence is that the ancient Britons had a particular predilection for deities whose incarnations were thought of as superhuman men and women with horns upon their heads. This liking for bulls and stags and human figures with the attributes and appearance of horned animals permeates the ancient world from Britain to the continent, across the Middle East and even as far as India. It may no coincidence that this is the area of the Indo-Europeans, from whose language almost all the modern European and South Asian languages are descended. It is hardly surprising that their folklore and mythology should similarly have influenced the countries to which their tribes spread in prehistoric times. The image of the horned god Cernunnos, for example, has been identified with the Lord of the Animals, a figure from Indian legend. This is not the whole story though. The Indo-Europeans migrated across Europe, Iran and India about 6000 or 8000 years ago, but 20,000 years before that some of the basic mythic figures were already established in European consciousness. Let us begin by looking at a truly primal image, the hunted stag.

The stag has been a powerful mythic image or archetype in European and British folklore for at least 30,000 years and almost certainly a lot longer than that. In the Italian Palaeolithic site of Arene Candide on the Ligurian coast, a burial dating back to about 23,000 BC has been excavated. The body of an adolescent boy was interred in a cave; covered in red ochre and with four batons crafted from the antlers of an elk lying beside him. In the Grimaldi cave, also in Italy, an even older burial was found, with a number of pierced stag's teeth around the body, possibly the remains of a necklace. This burial took place 30,000 years ago. Similar burials have been discovered in other parts of Europe. In Scandinavia, at Skateholm in Sweden and Vedbaek in Denmark, prehistoric graves have been uncovered of both men and women who have been laid to rest with deer antlers either under their heads or lying next to them.

What was the significance of the deer for the prehistoric people of Europe? For one thing, it was a source of useful materials for the hunter-gatherers who populated this continent before the advent of farming and the more settled lifestyle which became the norm during the Neolithic or New Stone Age. They hunted it for the meat, but also for the skin, which would have been used to make clothes and leather thongs. The antlers were very useful too. Most of the flint mining and building of monuments was carried out by means of picks and shovels made from deer antlers or shoulder blades. Harpoons, spearheads and needles could also be produced from the antlers, once they had been softened in water. It seems only to have been the stags which were hunted and killed. There was apparently a taboo on hunting the does; presumably because this would have caused the herd to die out after a year or two. We can gain some idea of how the deer was seen by early man if we look at the remnants of the nomadic tribes which still linger on in the far north of Europe. The Sami or Laplanders have a symbiotic relationship with the herds of reindeer which they tend. They eat reindeer meat, drink reindeer milk, use the antlers to make knife handles and toggles, the excrement as fuel for their fires, the fur to make clothes and tents. Their association with the reindeer is roughly analogous to the close relationship which the Native Americans had with the buffalo. There is reason to suppose that the early hunter-gatherers of Britain felt the same way about the deer. The stag is and has been for thousands of years in this country the tallest, swiftest and most powerful of all wild animals. It is a symbol of strength and virility. We hear a faint echo of this feeling when we talk of 'Stag Parties'.

When and how did this useful animal acquire a supernatural nature and become transmogrified into a god? The early stages in this process can be dated back at least 15,000 years. In the cave of Trois Frères in France are many paintings which were executed during the Palaeolithic era. Among them is one which has become known as 'the Sorcerer'. This shows either a god like Cernunnos or a man dressed up as a stag with antlers attached to or sprouting from his head. There has been some controversy about this image, which is really only known from the drawing made by Abbe Henri Breuil. Some have suggested that Breuil exaggerated the lines of the antlers in the image and that the Sorcerer as we know it owes as much to his drawing as to the original image. Recent work in the caves though confirms that the antlers are actually there, incised into the very rock upon which they were painted.

There are three basic interpretations of this strange picture. The first is that it shows some creature like a werewolf captured at the very moment of transformation from man to stag. The second is that this shows a god of some sort. The third possibility is that we are seeing a picture of a man dressing up in a stag's skin and antlers in order either to disguise himself so that he can stalk and kill deer or for the purpose acting in a charade of a successful hunt so that the real hunt might be blessed with good fortune. This interpretation would make this picture a representation of a ceremony of sympathetic magic.

That this is indeed what is depicted in the cave of Trois Frères has been confirmed by discoveries in the English county of Yorkshire at a place called Starr Carr. Ten thousand years ago there was a lake in this part of England. The lake dried up thousands of years ago, but the remains of the settlement which once flourished upon the shore of this long vanished lake still remain. The people who lived here were hunters and fishermen. They built houses or at least long-term shelters here and also a pier or jetty of the sort seen at Vauxhall in London. The pattern of finds leads archaeologists to think that many artefacts made from the antlers of red deer were thrown into the water as ritual sacrifices, just as we have seen with other bodies of water, such as the Thames in London. Among the things recovered were large numbers of barbed spear points carved from antler and also 33 masks or headpieces fashioned from the skulls of red deer.

The so-called 'frontlets' which had been produced by cutting away the top of deer skulls, leaving the antlers in place, had holes drilled in them. These were either eyeholes or holes to allow these frontlets to be attached to the head of one of the people living at the settlement. The appearance would thus have been uncannily similar to the Sorcerer of Trois Frères. There has been a good deal of discussion about whether these items were used to enable a hunter to stalk a deer closely or if they might have been used in rituals. The fact that the antlers had been cut down to manageable proportions suggests that they were not intended to disguise a deer hunter. That they had been ritually deposited in the open water also lends support to the idea of a ritual or ceremonial purpose.

Magic rituals are still performed to this day in order to endure success in the hunt. The Kalahari bush people, for example, dress up in this way, with one member of the ceremony taking the part of the animal and allowing himself to be surrounded and overpowered by those playing the part of the hunters. Nor do we need to travel as far as the Kalahari Desert to study ancient hunting ceremonies of this kind. An example is to be found in England itself, at the small village of Abbots Bromley, which is in the north of England and lies midway between Stafford and Burton-on-Trent.

Early on the morning of the Monday after the first Sunday following 4 September, a group of men collect six sets of very old reindeer antlers from the local church. They then process through the village and the surrounding farms until it is dark. In addition to those carrying the reindeer horns, there are other characters, such as the fool, a man dressed as a woman, the hobby horse and the bowman. A highly stylised dance takes place at intervals, in which the men carrying the reindeer horns pretend to face off in an imitation of the rutting displays of stags. At one point, the bowman 'hunts' the reindeer and fires imaginary arrows at them. This looks very much like the sort of sympathetic magic which is to be found in primitive, hunter-gatherer societies, designed to ensure success in the hunt.

It was fashionable a few years ago to dismiss the Abbots Bromley horn dance as being a Tudor invention. Certainly, the wooden posts to which the antlers are secured are from no later than the sixteenth century. In 1980, however, one set of antlers was in urgent need of repair. Permission was obtained to carbon date them at the same time and a date was obtained that showed that this set of antlers had been around for a thousand years or so, since about AD 1065, in fact. This tends to suggest that the dance is a very ancient indeed and may well represent a pre-Christian, perhaps even pre-Bronze Age tradition of magical ritual.

Although it was suppressed in the late nineteenth century, something of the same sort once took place annually in London itself. It was called the Charlton Horn Fair and it was celebrated across a part of London with very strong connections to the prehistoric ritual landscape, from Bermondsey in South London to the village of Charlton.

The Charlton Horn Fair was an altogether wilder and less picturesque business than the dance at Abbots Bromley. Writing in the early eighteenth century, Daniel Defoe had this to say of it:

Charleton, a village famous, or rather infamous for the yearly collected rabble of mad-people, at Horn-Fair; the rudeness of which I cannot but think, is such as ought to be suppressed, and indeed in a civiliz'd well govern'd nation, it may well

be said to be unsufferable. The mob indeed at that time take all kinds of liber-
ties, and the women are especially impudent for that day; as if it was a day that
justify'd the giving themselves a loose to all manner of indecency and immodesty.

The Horn Fair was held on 18 October and the procession started from Cuckold's
Point, which was a bend in the river, just before it reaches Tower Bridge. A tall
pole stood on the foreshore, surmounted by a pair of antlers. All those who took
part in the procession to Charlton wore horns of various kinds upon their heads.
These varied from ram's horns to sets of antlers. They passed through Greenwich,
once such an integral part of London's ritual landscape, before descending upon
the normally peaceful little village of Charlton. There was also, as with the Abbots
Bromley dance, a lot of cross dressing. At the fair, various articles carved from
horn were sold. Just as with Herne the Hunter, a medieval legend was later con-
cocted to explain away the Charlton Horn Fair, but its form and nature suggest
strongly a pre-Christian ceremony of some kind.

Another feature of this procession is that it started from Bermondsey and followed the river towards Woolwich. Wooden trackways, similar to the famous
Sweet Track in Somerset, have been discovered along this route and carbon dated
to 4000 BC. This may be a coincidence. It may, on the other hand, suggest that
6000 years ago there was enough ritual and religious activity in that area to justify
the enormous exertion required to build a wooden road across the mudflats and
marshes of this part of South London. It is hard to imagine what the purpose
would otherwise have been for such a track; there is little evidence of towns or
other settlements in the area having been in existence 6000 years ago.

Animals with horns and antlers seemed to have occupied a particular and venerated place in the minds of our ancient ancestors. In Western Europe it was the
deer, but in the Mediterranean area and further east it was the bull, which was held
in especial regard, almost certainly for similar reasons of speed, strength and sexual
prowess. Little wonder then that the chief god of whom we have definite knowledge in this country was the horned god who came to be known as Cernunnous.

The actual name of this god, Cernunnos, is known from only a single inscription. It is on a stone pillar which in the eighteenth century was found to be
incorporated into the foundations of Notre-Dame Cathedral in Paris. The so-
called Pillar of the Mariners was carved by Gaulish sailors, most probably in AD
14. It depicts a number of gods, some Roman and others Celtic. The most prominent is a man with antlers sprouting from his head. Torcs are hanging from the
antlers and, judging by what remains of the pillar, he is sitting in a cross-legged
position, rather in the South Asian style which has become associated with the
Buddha. The inscription identifies him as Cernunnos.

A similar figure is to be found on the Gundestrap Cauldron which was recovered from a bog in Denmark. This silver-gilt vessel has been dated to a century
or so before the birth of Christ and was dismantled and then deposited in the

bog, presumably as a votive offering. The workmanship is Thracian, from the region between Greece and Turkey, but the subject matter of the chased images is pure Celtic.

One figure in particular catches the attention. It is man with the antlers of a stag and he is sitting cross-legged on the ground. In another panel, he brandishes two stags, one in each hand. Without a doubt, this is the horned god Cernunnos. That both he and the representation from the Pillar of the Mariners should show him sitting cross-legged like some yogi adept is intriguing. A seal from the Indian city of Mohenjo Daro shows Pasuptei, the Lord of the Animals, in the same pose. It is at least possible that these are both images of the same archetypal figure. Another similarity is that the figure on the Gundestrap Cauldron is also wearing a torc.

Returning to London, it is curious to note that the traditions of the deer being involved in worship and sacrifice lingered on until the sixteenth century. Significantly, the place where such things were last recorded was at St Paul's Cathedral, which, as we saw earlier, was probably the site of earlier religious sanctuaries dating before the Roman conquest. We have already seen that many skulls of deer, boars and oxen were dug up during the reign of Edward I when work was being carried out on the old St Paul's Cathedral. Before the Great Fire, a building connected with the old cathedral was called the 'Camera Dianae' or Diana's Chambers. This stood in Benet's Lane and was the official residence for the canons of St Paul's. Writing in the late sixteenth century, the noted antiquarian William Camden said:

> That there stood in old time a Temple of Diana in this place some have conjectured, and arguments there are to make this their conjecture good. Certain old houses adjoining are in the ancient records of the Church called Diana's Chamber, and in the church-yard, while Edward the First reigned, an incredible number of Ox-heads were digged up, as we find in our Annals, which the common sort at that time made a wondering at, as the Sacrifices of Gentiles, and the learned know that Tauropolia were celebrated in the honour of Diana. I myself also when I was a boy have seen a stag's head sticking upon a spear-top (a ceremony suiting well with the Sacrifices of Diana) carried roundabout within the very Church in solemn pomp and procession, and with a great noise of Horne-blows. And that Stag or Hart which they of the house de Bawde in Essex did present for certain lands that there held, as I have heard say, the Priests of this Church, arrayed in their sacred vestments and wearing garlands of flowers upon their heads, were wont to receive at the steps of the quire.

Priests with garlands of flowers on their heads, a stag's head being paraded on a spear, even accounting for the changes in church ritual since the time of Elizabeth I – this does sound rather more like a primitive rite than a Christian church service. John Stowe, another contemporary writer, said of this ceremony:

the buck being brought up the steps of St Paul's church, at the hour of the procession, the dean and chapter being apparelled in copes and vestments, with garlands of roses on their heads, they sent the body of the buck to baking, and had the head fixed upon a pole, borne before cross in the procession.

It has to be said that Christopher Wren, who supervised the digging of the foundations for the present cathedral, dismissed the idea that any previous temple had stood on Ludgate Hill. At the time that the new St Paul's was being built, there was much discussion among scholars as to the whether or not a pre-Christian temple had once been there. Dr Woodward, a contemporary of Wren's, had in his possession a bronze statue of Diana which had been found buried near the Deanery. He claimed that this was indicative of a temple or sanctuary dedicated to Diana. Sir Christopher would have none of it. He said, talking of Geoffrey of Monmouth's story that temples to both Apollo and Diana had once existed in London:

> I must assert that having changed all the foundations of old St Paul's, and upon that occasion having rummaged all the ground thereabouts and being very desirous of finding the footsteps of such a temple I could not find any and therefore can give no more credit to Diana than Apollo.

This sounds definite enough. Wren found plenty of burials beneath the charred ruins old St Paul's, but no sign of a temple. For many, this has been enough to put an end to the idea of temple to Diana on the summit of Ludgate Hill, but more recent discoveries have reopened the question.

In 1830 an altar to Diana was found in Fosters Lane during the rebuilding of Goldsmiths Hall. The goddess was accompanied by a dog and is portrayed as reaching back into her quiver for an arrow. Presumably, she is about to fire at a stag. This was only 200 yards from the cathedral. A little later, in 1841, traces of a Roman mosaic pavement were found near St Paul's and since then other Roman brickwork has come to light. In 1988, while the amphitheatre beneath the Guildhall was being restored, a lead 'curse tablet' was found. This provided written evidence for the cult of Diana in Londinium. Curse tablets were appeals to the gods and goddesses. They were like letters, posted into rivers wells or left at shrines. They were part of the contract of religion which we looked at in Chapter 3. The one found beneath the Guildhall says: 'I give to the goddess Diana my headgear and scarf less one-third. If anyone has done this, I give him, and through me let him be unable to live.'

This is almost conclusive proof that there was a temple dedicated to Diana in Londinium. Where we see other such curse tablets promising to give something to a named god or goddess, these have invariably been deposited at the temples or shrines of that deity. The only way that the author of the curse tablet quoted above would have been able to give Diana a third of the value of the headscarf would have been by giving something equal to this value to a sanctuary associated with the goddess.

We cannot know how those living in ancient Europe thought of their gods. Their mythology is utterly lost to us, except insofar as we can observe later customs and extrapolate backwards, a hazardous and uncertain undertaking. The earliest religious beliefs in England of which we know are those of the Celts who lived here when the Romans invaded. Although they shared some beliefs with those living in mainland Europe, the inhabitants of Britain were in some ways unique in their beliefs and practices.

The Celts of whom Caesar wrote had only been in Britain for a few centuries. They were of the group known as the Belgae and had crossed the Channel between 500 and 200 BC. This was just one of many successive waves of immigration from the continent. There were primitive hominids living in the area which would later become London as early as half a million years ago. Their hand axes have been found in central London. Later, bands of hunter-gatherers from Europe crossed the North Sea, which was a grassy plain at that time, and settled in this country. Many thousands of years later, after the end of the last ice age, groups of farmers came here to settle. This was around 3500 BC and their society grew and developed for some thousands of years. In mainland Europe a nation had emerged called variously the Celts or Keltoi. As they expanded in search of new territory, they eventually reached the coast of Belgium and France. From there it was a short journey to Britain and 2500 years ago they began to come here from Europe. It was not an invasion in the strictest sense of the word. There may certainly have been skirmishes with those already living here, as attested by archaeological evidence, but these newcomers brought also new technology and ways of doing things.

These waves of newcomers have provided the British with a series of stock mythic figures. Everybody is familiar with King Arthur, but he is simply one avatar or incarnation of a very British figure, the leader of a band who resist the invaders from Europe. When the Romans came, we had Caratacus, the noble Briton fighting a hopeless battle to protect his homeland. Five hundred years later, Arthur, the Romanised Celt, fights a similar battle against the Saxon invaders. Another 500 years and Hereward the Wake, the Anglo-Dane, is fighting the Norman invaders. Robin Hood belongs to the same mythic group.

We have touched upon the awkward fact that all our accounts of Celtic pagan religion are from classical writers. Some of these writers may well have added their own gloss to the stories which they had heard; stories which might well have been themselves exaggerated or inaccurate. Bearing this in mind and making allowance for the prejudices of those writers of antiquity, what can we say about the early Britons and their religion?

We have Julius Caesar to thank for much of our knowledge about Celtic religion. Writing in *The Gallic Wars*, he described the beliefs of those whom he and his army conquered in both France and Britain. Caesar at least had first-hand experience of the nations of whom he wrote. He said that the Celts believed in the immortality of the soul and that it was this which made the Celtic warriors seem almost indifferent to their own deaths in battle. It does not appear to have occurred to him that this might also have been because they were fighting for their freedom and the right to determine their own affairs. This is not a perspective which one expects to find in even the most enlightened Roman historian. Caesar also claimed that the Celts believed the head to be the seat of the soul and also that human sacrifice was carried out under the rule of the Druids.

As far as the importance attached to the head is concerned, there is no reason to doubt what Caesar says. That the Celts were enthusiastic head-hunters is amply borne out by archaeological evidence. Not only individual skulls, but also statues of deities holding severed heads and, from mainland Europe, a gruesome ceremonial archway with niches for decapitated heads to be placed in, all testify to the reverence which the Celts felt towards the heads of their enemies. According to other classical writers, the severed heads of enemies were accorded great respect. They were preserved in cedar oil and passed round to be admired at feasts. In Chapter 6 we will look at both the cult of dead and also the fascination with the severed head.

Caesar apparently believed that the Celts worshipped the same gods as the Romans, although under different names. Camulos, the Celtic god of war, for example, he identified with Mars. It will be remembered that the plaque found in London which mentioned Camulos called him Mars-Camulos. This strongly suggests that the two gods were widely thought to be one and the same, at least by Romans. Nor was this the only example of Celtic and Roman gods being thought to be different incarnations of the same personage. The fact that a road had been built linking Colchester with London in this way may be significant. Colchester was, before the coming of the Romans, a town dedicated to Camulos, a Celtic deity. This is the origin of the Roman name for the town: Camulodunum – City of Camulos. Camulos was shown in Celtic coins as bearing horns, another example of the recurring image of a horned god. Could the purpose of the road leading from Camulodunum to London have been to allow worshippers to travel to a place dedicated to the patron god of their city?

What can we say about the gods and goddesses who were venerated in London itself? How might the modes of worship have affected the landscape and left physical traces which we can still discern beneath the streets of the modern city? A stone's throw from Duke Street Hill and Southwark Cathedral, on the south bank of the Thames, was a Romano-Celtic temple. This might be a good point at which to distinguish between the British temple-building tradition and that of the Romans and Greeks.

Classical temples are structures somewhat like the Parthenon in Athens: impressive stone buildings with fluted columns. There are one or two examples of these in Britain; most notably in Colchester and at Bath. Most temples though are the rather more modest buildings known as Romano-Celtic temples. These are typically square buildings, about the size of a chapel or small church. Many were erected over existing sites of religious significance to the native inhabitants of this country.

At Harlow, a town near London, a Romano-Celtic temple has been thoroughly excavated in a leisurely fashion seldom possible in London itself, where any dig has to be conducted with the developers of the building site breathing down the necks of the archaeologists. The temple was built, as was common, on the bank of a river, in this case the Stort. Associated with the temple itself were a large number of freshly minted coins, clearly deposited during the Roman occupation as votive offerings at the temple. Beneath the Roman structure, though, was found traces of an earlier round wooden building, which had stood here before being demolished and replaced by the grander stone temple. Iron Age coins from before the Roman invasion were also found, indicating that this site had been in use at least some centuries before the Romano-Celtic temple was built. Beneath these, however, were found Bronze Age burials of cremated human remains. This pattern of continued use of a sacred site for thousands of years has been found elsewhere in Britain and is almost certainly a feature of the sites in London as well. The problem is that because archaeological investigations must usually be carried out at breakneck speed in the capital, due to commercial constraints, it is seldom possible to look at every layer of the past in this way.

These Romano-Celtic temple complexes were usually dedicated to gods who combined the attributes of both a Roman and local deity. It seems likely that they are really a natural extension of the ritual landscape which dated from the Neolithic period or even earlier. It is through looking at inscriptions and cult statues from sites such as this that we are able to reconstruct the gods and goddesses who were venerated by the natives of Britain. It should be possible to disentangle them from the Roman deities whom they perhaps found it politic to accord at least lip service during the military occupation of their homeland.

According to the plaque which was uncovered in Southwark in 2002, the temple which stood there was associated in some way with to Mars-Camulos. As we saw, he was generally depicted with horns on his head. Just outside London, in Hertfordshire, a Romano-Celtic temple was excavated which was used for the worship of Mars-Alator. Alator means 'huntsman'. South of London, Apollo the sun god was worshipped as Apollo-Cunomaglos, or Prince of the Hounds, another hunting related reference.

The Romans found it easy to see how those in the countries which they had conquered might already be familiar with the gods of Rome, simply knowing them by other names and this was truer than either side knew. The pantheon of Roman gods shared a common Indo-European origin with the gods of Britain. It was hardly surprising that some of them seemed so similar in appearance and attributes.

Bearing in mind what we have seen earlier about the continuity of worship at sites which may date back thousands of years, it seems likely that the temples built in London during the Roman occupation were erected on pre-existing shrines or places of pilgrimage. In other words, the Southwark temple was probably placed in this part of London because this was a spot sacred to a horned god, in this case Camulos. It will be remembered that a statue of a hunting god was recovered from a well shaft not far from the Southwark temple, beneath the modern cathedral. This god too has a connection with hunting; he is accompanied by two fierce-looking hounds. In Chapter 2 we saw that another Romano-Celtic temple once stood on high ground in Greenwich Park. *Colour plate 7* shows how it might have looked. This temple also has a connection with horns and hunting. During excavations at the site an almost life-size arm of a statue or cult figure was unearthed. It was female, draped in robes and the hand had been drilled for the attachment of some implement or tool. The assumption was that this was part of a statue of Diana, divine huntress and sister of Apollo. The temple in Greenwich was probably dedicated to this goddess, whose worship was inextricably linked with the hunting of deer. Her cult animals, those sacrificed in her honour, included both boars and deer. It will, of course, be recalled that the skulls of these animals were found in their hundreds during the building work at the old St Paul's Cathedral; an indication that Ludgate Hill was also once a holy place for the worshippers of Diana. It is possible to work out indirectly just who was being honoured at various sites by the nature of the bones found there. At Uley near Cirencester, for example, was a temple to Mercury. His cult animals were the cockerel and ram. A statue of the god at this temple had a ram and cockerel at his feet. Over 90 per cent of the animal bones dug up there were those of those two animals. These bones alone would have provided strong evidence for the worship of Mercury at this site. In a similar way, the bones of deer and boar found at the top of Ludgate Hill are, even in the absence of other evidence, indicative of the worship of Diana there.

Now Diana may have been a goddess imported by the Romans, but many of her characteristics were familiar to the Celts and before them, probably to those who lived in Britain thousands of years earlier. She was associated with wild country and in particular oak groves. The oak was, of course, a sacred tree in this country long before the arrival of Roman culture. It was sacred not only to Diana, but to the Druids who performed their rituals in oak groves. It seems likely that Diana fitted in so readily with the religious practices of the Britons because they already knew her under a different name. The hunter of the stag had been a religious archetype across Europe for tens of thousands of years. Diana, with her bow and pack of hounds, would not have seemed at all strange to those living in this country 2000 years ago. The only novelty might have been her gender, but Celtic society placed far more importance upon women than did other, supposedly more civilised, nations of that time. A female hunter of stags with a bow and pack of hunting dogs would have been quite an acceptable image.

We have seen that in Roman London hunter gods and goddesses were known under various names. We have also seen the horned god mentioned in dedicatory inscriptions from a temple. What other deities were known at that time?

We know for sure of at least two other temples in London, apart from those already mentioned. Both have a connection with horns. A jug was uncovered which was inscribed '*Londini as fanum Isidis*', 'At London, by the temple of Isis'. We have seen that the Romans were not at all averse to adopting other gods and goddesses and worshipping them alongside their own deities. The case of the Egyptian goddess Isis is rather special, though. Her worship spread contemporaneously with Christianity across the Greco-Roman world. So popular was this goddess that some of her titles and attributes were seized by the Christians and bestowed upon Mary, the mother of Christ. 'Queen of Heaven' and 'Star of the Sea' are today recognised titles of the Virgin Mary; both originated with Isis. The image of Isis nursing the infant Horus upon her lap is also eerily familiar to those steeped in Christian iconography. It might have provided the template for the Madonna and child featured in countless Christian paintings and sculptures.

For our purposes, there are two important things to note about the goddess Isis, whose temple stood in London. Firstly, of course, she was a female deity, rather than a male. Secondly, she was depicted with horns emerging from her head. These had a dual significance. As shown in sculptures, these horns are clearly those of a cow or bull, but Isis was also goddess of the moon and the horns are also suggestive of the crescent moon.

The other temple which we know of was discovered shortly after the Second World War. It is a Mithraeum and it once stood on the bank of the Walbrook (see *colour plates 3 & 4*). Mithras was a semi-divine man who triumphed by slaying a bull and allowing its blood to flow out on to the earth. Sculptures of bulls were displayed in these temples. The iconography of the cult of Mithras has some features which might show a resonance with the religious practices in this country before the Romans. In carvings, Mithras is accompanied by two men bearing flaming torches. One is called Cautes and the other Cautopates. Cautes is depicted holding his torch aloft, while Cautopates is holding his pointing downwards. The most common interpretation of these two companions is that they represent either dawn and dusk or the spring and autumn equinoxes. If so, then this would be a mighty god who vanquishes a horned animal, with the personifications of two liminal, temporal zones on either side of him.

We know that the Roman sun god Apollo was linked at a Romano-Celtic place of worship with Cunomaglos, the Lord of the Hounds. This is seen in an inscription from a temple in Wiltshire, which says: '*DEO APOLLINI CVNOMAGLO COROTICA IVTI [F] VSLM*'. Roughly translated, this means, 'to the god Apollo Cunomaglos; Coroticus, son of Lutus willingly performs his vow'. This is one of the contracts which we looked at in Chapter 3. Presumably, Coroticus asked some favour of the god and, when it was granted, he showed his thanks by a contribution to the temple, either financial or in the form of a new statue.

The threads seem to be coming together in our understanding of the gods and goddesses of prehistoric Britain. We know that deity was associated with horns, whether of deer, ram or bull. The image of the half man, half horned beast is found across much of the ancient world from as far back as 30,000 years. Connected with this is the hunt as an archetype. Diana hunts and slays deer, Mithras kills the bull, the skulls of sacrificed horned animals are found in graves and on the sites of temples. With the hunt go dogs. Apollo is conflated with Cunomaglos, Lord of the Hounds. Dogs' skulls and skeletons are placed in wells as votive offerings. Mars is linked to Alator, also a huntsman.

This powerful theme of chasing and killing horned animals and the confusion between deity and the horned animal argue for an immensely ancient origin of these images. For almost 10,000 years, European culture has been pastoral or industrial, rather than that of hunter-gatherers. The Neolithic period in Europe began in Greece about 7000 BC and from there spread across the rest of the continent. As agriculture spread, so too did the keeping of domestic animals for food. Hunting might have continued as a means to supplement the meat from sheep, pigs and cattle, but it had nothing like the central and vital importance which was the case in the Palaeolithic or Old Stone Age.

The religious framework in Britain before the Roman invasion was broadly established shortly after the retreat of the glaciers, 18,000 years ago. The powerful mythic images of the bull and the stag could hardly have emerged before that time as the fauna of Europe was radically different. The special status of dogs, skeletons of which are found in graves, henges and wells, could not have been around for more than 12,000 years or so. This is when the domestication of dogs from the selective breeding of tame wolves is widely supposed to have begun.

I say that the images of the horned prey animals could not have been extant until the glaciers had been gone for many years, but it is just possible that the archetype of the mighty horned animal that was hunted could have originated with the mammoth. Its huge curved tusks are almost precisely similar to horns and it might be that the earliest image of this sort to impress itself on the prehistoric mind was that of the enormous shaggy creature with the fearsome curved tusks.

Primitive people frequently take particular animals as the totem for their tribes or communities. Sometimes this can be a dangerous animal; the jaguar of South America is a good example of this, or the leopard of Africa. Others take an animal that is very useful to them, such as the fish or deer.

At the site of Lepenski Vir, on the banks of the River Danube in former Yugoslavia, a 7000-year-old village has been excavated. The inhabitants lived by hunting and fishing; the revolution of Neolithic farming had yet to reach them. There are two outstanding features of this Stone Age community. First, every home had both a hearth and an altar. The domestic and religious were thus indistinguishable; each home was also a temple. We saw something similar at Catal Huyuk which was roughly contemporaneous with Lepenski Vir.

The other aspect of Lepenski Vir which bears upon our discussion is the nature of the idols and sacrifices made in the homes. The villagers held sacred three animals: the stag, the dog and the fish. Piscine statues are found all over the site and buried beneath the altars are remains of sacrifices. These consist entirely of the three animals mentioned above. The people at Lepenski Vir were on the cusp of the coming pastoralism of the Neolithic and the hunter-gatherer societies of the Palaeolithic. They were poised midway between the old ways and the new, in that that although they lived in a settled community, they also lived by hunting wild animals. The only domesticated animal known to them was the dog. Both their prey animals, the stag and fish, were held in reverence and so too was the animal which helped in the hunt: their tame dogs.

At places like Catal Huyuk and Lepenski Vir, we can see the salient points which defined the communities of Britain before the arrival of the Romans. On the one hand is the complete melding of religious and secular life, the blurring of the boundaries between the world of spirits and the real living world. Secondly is the obsession with the stag and the dog, the hunter and the quarry. There can be no doubt that the preoccupation with stags and dogs which we see again and again in this country's ancient past is a throwback to the time before the advent of farming, when the acquisition of meat meant not selecting a fat sheep whose throat only needed to be cut, but setting off with a pack of hounds in search of some horned animals to hunt down and kill.

The legend of the Wild Hunt, another British archetype, is a relic of this: the confused mass of baying hounds and armed men in pursuit of the stag or other quarry. Herne the Hunter leads the hunt in some parts of the country, a semi-divine being with antlers sprouting from his skull. He looks like one of the shamans from Starr Carr or the sorcerer from the Trois Frères cave.

With the advent of farming, hunting changed from a desperately important mission to ensure the survival of the group into a means of supplementing the diet of wheat and butchered domestic livestock. In time it metamorphosed from essential skill to hobby, as is the case in the western world today. In the British Isles, though, the ancient respect for the hunter and his obsessive devotion to the quarry survived the arrival of the Neolithic Age with its agriculture. When men and women wanted to return to basics, it was to the hunter they looked.

The Celts in Britain had only arrived in the country a few centuries before Julius Caesar landed in Kent. Indeed, some of them, the Belgae, had come within living memory. It is strange then that the religion of the Celts, Druidism, should be rooted in this country and not in mainland Europe. Caesar was in no doubt that Britain was the centre of Druidism, which rather suggests that this was not some essentially Celtic belief system. If that were the case, then the centre for it would have been in mainland Europe. If Druidism was a religion of the Celts which they had brought with them when they came to Britain, one would have thought that those wishing to learn more of it would be obliged to travel back to Europe, perhaps France, to learn more of it. It is also rather odd that the main base of Druidism should have been as far from the Celtic homeland as it was possible to get, on the Welsh island of Anglesey. Perhaps Druidism was not quite such a new religion as we might think. It could be that those who we call Druids were actually the practitioners of a religion older than anything that the civilised world of the late Iron Age knew about: the cult of the hunter and the hunted.

If Caesar was right about this, and it is hard to see why he should have made it up, the religion of the Celts in Europe was exported there from this country. Did Britain perhaps retain older traditions in these matters; traditions which had been forgotten in Europe itself? Could it be the case that those from Europe recognised that in Britain was to be found the authentic and ancient religion based upon myths which had been blurred and obscured by the more sophisticated societies of Rome and Greece? Such a belief system would probably feature the hunter and the stag, the importance of the severed head and also the immortality of the soul.

We know for certain of four temples in Roman London, at least two of which had their roots centuries before the invasion. These are Greenwich, Southwark, the temple of Isis at an unknown location and the temple of Mithras on the bank of the Walbrook. We are also able to deduce the existence of a number of other temples, for example those which we believe lie beneath St Paul's Cathedral and Westminster Abbey. It is hard not to notice that in almost every single case these temples were connected with hunters and horned beasts. The temple at Southwark was dedicated to Mars-Camulos. Camulos was a horned god. The temple at Greenwich had a cult statue to Diana, goddess of the hunt. The temple of Mithras was connected with the slaying of a horned animal and we know that there was also a temple to Isis, who was depicted as a woman with horns on her head. Of the possible other temples, we can say this. There may well have been a shrine on the site of present day Southwark Cathedral; there was at least a well there and a Roman building and the statue of a hunter god was found in the well. Legends from as far back as the times of the Saxons hint that on Ludgate Hill was a temple devoted to Diana, goddess of the hunt. The remains of stags and boars, her cult animals, have been found there. And at Westminster, those same old legends tell of a temple to Apollo. Apollo was, according to an inscription found in Wiltshire, identified and worshipped by some as Apollo-Cunomaglos, Lord of the Hounds and a mighty hunter. And near to London in Hertfordshire was a Romano-Celtic shrine of Mars-Alator, *alator* meaning hunter. It must seem, even to the most unbiased observer, as though a definite pattern is emerging.

The thesis is that in Britain, isolated from the mainstream of European culture, traces of an older belief system endured. Whatever lip service was paid to new beliefs imported by the Romans or Celts, the devotion in this country was to the vital spirits of the hunter and his prey; personified and in some cases deified as a hunter who combines the essential features of both man and beast, hunter and quarry. London was the natural home of this primitive religion and it was linked with other beliefs such as the cult of the dead and the reverence felt for the severed human head.

6

Severed Heads and the Cult of the Dead

To the Celts who lived in Britain, the head was without doubt the most important part of the body. It was the seat of the soul and human personality and as such deserved special respect. This attention to the skull in not just a European tradition. We have looked at Lepenski Vir and Catal Huyuk, two of the first towns; we turn now to the oldest city in the world, Jericho. Jericho was already 5000 years old when Joshua besieged it about 1500 BC. This is a Neolithic town; 4000 years older than the cities of nearby Sumer. The first people who lived in Jericho practised a strange form of ancestor worship. They coated the skulls of their dead relatives with plaster and then sculpted the likeness of the deceased. These grisly reminders would occupy an honoured position in the homes of Jericho's citizens.

Again, at Catal Huyuk, we have already seen in that ancient town reflections of some of the themes at which we have looked: the stag, the bull's horns and dead people interred in the homes of the living. Some wall paintings also show headless human figures. Even here, in the earliest urban centre in the world, we see evidence for a cult involving the human head. Over and over again, from the Middle East to the westernmost parts of Europe, we see a preoccupation with heads which have been removed from the body.

Returning to this country, there are any number of examples of prehistoric headless corpses. In 1823, William Buckland, who became famous as the discoverer of the Megalosuarus, carried out a dig at a site on the Gower Peninsula in Wales. At Goat's Hole cave in Paviland, Buckland found the remains of a prehistoric human skeleton which he wrongly identified as being that of a female. The body had been liberally sprinkled with red ochre and was known for years as the 'Red Lady' of Paviland. Actually, the skeleton was that of a man in his late twenties and dated back to around 24,000 BC. This burial had one very curious and unexplained feature: the head was missing.

In London, there is abundant evidence for the cult of the sacred head. In addition to the decapitated heads found in the Walbrook, the Thames too has yielded up many skulls. Significantly, these are seldom accompanied by other human bones. At least one well in London, that in Queen Street, was found to contain a human head, while others had dogs heads buried behind their walls. In 2007, building works at St Martin-in-the-Fields church at Trafalgar Square unearthed a Roman coffin containing a skeleton. The head was missing. Causewayed enclosures too, not infrequently have human skulls buried in their ditches, along with the skulls of other animals such as dogs and deer. That human heads are found in ritual structures dating from the early Neolithic gives us reason to think that the Celtic cult of the sacred head was not something specific to their culture but more the latest manifestation of a very ancient idea.

Perhaps examining the practices of the Celts in London will shed some light upon the earlier ideas about human heads and their importance. The Celts thought that the head was the part of the body where the person's soul was to be found and as such deserved special consideration. Their collecting of heads from enemies was not a simple case of trophy hunting, but a mark of respect. It is true that in some cultures the head of an enemy will be mistreated, kicked around like a football and have all sorts of insults and indignities heaped upon it, but this was most decidedly not the case with the Celts. A classical writer, Diodorus Siculus, said:

> They cut off the heads of enemies slain in battle and attach them to the necks of their horses. These blood stained spoils they hand over to their attendants and carry off as booty, while striking up a paean and singing a song of victory, and they nail up these first fruits upon their houses just as those who lay low wild animals in certain kinds of hunting. They embalm in cedar oil the heads of the most distinguished enemies and preserve them carefully in a chest, and display them with pride to strangers, saying that, for this head, one of their ancestors, or his father, or the man himself, refused a large sum of money. They say that some of them boast that they refused the weight of the head in gold.

Archaeological evidence has confirmed this description. A skull from this period was found to have traces of cedar oil on it.

On the mainland of Europe a Celtic temple had stone doorposts with niches for human heads to be displayed and, as in Britain, the number of individual skulls which turn up without their bodies is astonishing. From France too, comes a Celtic statue of a strange beast holding in its claws two decapitated heads.

The decapitated head is a *leitmotif* of Celtic art. Rows of heads decorate shields and chariot fittings, individual heads are used on buckets and scabbards. Stone sculptures of disembodied heads are also common. They are carved on standing stones, worked into horse trappings and feature on jewellery. There can be not the slightest doubt that the Celts had a thing about heads which were not attached to bodies. Just as with other pre-Christian practices, it is possible to observe this pre-occupation with severed heads in early Christian churches. Throughout Britain, a large number of old churches have worked disembodied heads into their decorations, either as gargoyles or simply ceiling bosses and embellishments on fonts.

That the casting of human heads into the Thames in London was a fairly common event is indicated in two ways. First, the skulls alone are found, with no accompanying bones, even the jawbone. The discolouration of the skulls often suggests that they had been exposed to the open air for some time without being covered with flesh. This effectively does away with one theory, that the skulls had simply been washed into the rivers by floods at cemeteries. This discolouration is further evidence for the practice of excarnation, which was dealt with in Chapter 3. The second indication that something special was going on with heads is the number of face pots which have also been found in the Thames and its tributaries, in particular the Walbrook. These are ceramic vessels which have been shaped like heads, even down to having eyes, noses and mouths. The Romans frowned on human sacrifice and all the rituals associated with it. They certainly discouraged it in the countries which they occupied. It was one of the reasons why they suppressed Druidism in this country. It might be the face pots became a substitute method of offering up severed heads in Londinium during the occupation.

Face pots are first known from the Rhine valley and were introduced into Britain by the Roman army. Broken pieces of face pots have been washed up on the Thames foreshore, but nearly all the complete examples which have turned up have been found in the Walbrook valley. This is strongly suggestive that both the Walbrook and the face pots were part of some ritual behaviour which involved heads. In 1834, a bronze head of the emperor Hadrian was found in the Thames at London. This could be another aspect of the ritual deposition of heads in the river at this point.

Two sources of information which indicate a cult of the sacred head in London have been examined. These are archaeological evidence and the writings of classical authors who had observed the Celts. There is a third source, one which might contain direct memories of the cult of the sacred head. These are folk tales from Ireland and Wales, at least one of which refers to London. There is also a very strange custom which could be a case of the continuation of use in some specific ritual site which we have found to be so common in London.

The *Mabinogion* is a Welsh epic, a collection of legends and folktales which were first collected and written down as one book during the eleventh century. These stories are Celtic myths which had been passed down orally since before the Roman conquest. It is sometimes hard to tell when reading them whether the characters are gods, giants or mighty kings of the past. One of the stories concerns Bran and his sister Bronwen, son and daughter of Lyr, which are more familiar to us as the King Lear about whom Shakespeare wrote a play.

Bran was High King over all Britain. The King of Ireland asked for Bronwen's hand in marriage and when Bran consented, she went off to marry him. There were disputes between Bran and the Irish king and as a peace offering, Bran gave the Irish a magic cauldron which was capable of resurrecting the dead. Later, when he heard that his sister had been sent to work in the kitchens of the king's palace, Bran launched an invasion of Ireland. During the fighting, he was mortally wounded in his foot by a poisoned spear. He instructed his followers to cut off his head when he was dead and bury it beneath the White Mount in London. According to the legend, Bran's head talked throughout the journey to London, entertaining his companions with songs, anecdotes and stories. His head would, he told the men, provide magical protection for the country against enemies. Later on King Arthur had the head dug up. He wished that the protection of Britain should depend upon nobody but himself.

There are in this story elements of later legends. The magic vessel is the prototype for the Holy Grail. The reference to resurrection indicates a connection with Christianity. The king wounded in his foot is a motif found in the legend of the Fisher King and for Arthur, a Romanised Celt, to dig up the head of Bran and reject its protection suggests a reliance upon Christianity and rejection of faith in the Celtic gods.

We come now to some exceedingly odd coincidences. *Bran* means 'raven' in old Celtic. There is, of course, an old legend concerning this bird and the Tower of London, built right by Tower Hill. Tower Hill has been identified as the White Mount where Bran's head was buried. The legend has it that as long as there are ravens at the Tower, London will be safe from enemy invasion. Is this a garbled version of the tale told in the *Mabinogion*? The name 'Raven' and the ravens living close by the place where his head was buried must surely be connected in some way.

Important Christian places of worship have been built above sites which the Celts living in London regarded as sacred. This happened with Westminster Abbey, St Paul's Cathedral and many other places, and was a custom which others had followed. The Romans built their own shrines above holy places and no doubt the Celts in their turn had done the same. This is how newcomers stamp their authority upon a land. We must ask ourselves why, after conquering this country, William chose Tower Hill as the place to build his fortress. Did he know of the legend of Bran which made Tower Hill so important? Was there perhaps a shrine of some sort on the spot, perhaps near the healing spring which bubbled up near here?

Ravens are the birds which perched on the shoulder of Odin, chief of the Norse gods. He had two, called Thought and Memory, and they used to bring him the news from Midgard or Earth. We remember too the practice of excarnation as a way of preparing human corpses for final disposal. In some countries, the birds which would play a vital part in this process would be vultures; they are shown performing this role on wall paintings from Catal Huyuk. In Britain, the most likely birds to peck the flesh from corpses would be ravens and crows.

Some customs seem to have a habit of cropping up again and again in London, quite independently and seemingly by coincidence. The throwing of coins into a shaft at Southwark Cathedral was one such tradition which erupted after a gap of 1500 years or so as soon as a shaft leading to the world of the dead, as symbolised by an open coffin, was available. Something very much the same, although far more gruesome, seems to have taken place at both Tower Hill and Southwark.

We know that the Celts were keen head-hunters and that this obsession and veneration for decapitated heads was rooted far further back in the past than just Celtic culture. Heads were collected and displayed, some at least probably being supposed to have special powers as talismans. The story of Bran is a folk memory of this preoccupation with severed heads. That the White Mount at London is specifically linked to the story of a severed head, which makes it possible that this place had some sort of history of being involved with the cult of the sacred head. During the Middle Ages, a custom arose concerning this hill, which was after the Norman conquest and building of the Tower of London, known as Tower Hill. It became the chief place in London where beheadings were carried out. The decapitated heads of the monarch's enemies would afterwards be displayed on a bridge as a warning to others. This was trophy head-hunting on a regal scale!

Almost unbelievably, the custom of cutting off people's heads continued at Tower Hill until the middle of the eighteenth century. The last person to be deprived of his head in this way on Tower Hill was Lord Lovat on 9 April 1747. He had been involved in the Stuart uprising in Scotland against the Hanoverian kings of Britain. Although 80 years old, he was beheaded in public on Tower Hill after a brief trial for treason. The axe and block used for this execution are still displayed in the Tower of London. *Figure 12* shows the plaque which marks the place on Tower Hill where this execution took place.

The motif of the skull or decapitated head seems to crop up around Tower Hill in various unexpected places. In Seething Lane, for instance, five minutes' stroll from Tower Hill, is one of the most extraordinary sights in London. Even Charles Dickens, no stranger to the outlandish and grotesque in London, was impressed with the portal of St Olave's churchyard. In *The Uncommercial Traveller*, he describes it thus:

> One of my best loved churchyards, I call the churchyard of Saint Ghastly Grim. It is a small, small churchyard with a ferocious spiked iron gate like a jail. This gate is ornamented with skulls and crossbones larger than life, wrought in stone; thrust through and through with iron spears.

This strange gateway is still there and it looks like nothing so much as a celebration of the severed head. At the Iron Age Celtic sanctuary of Roquepertuse in France, a stone gateway guarded the entrance. It incorporated niches for the decapitated heads of enemy warriors. This portal looks hideous, with half a dozen skulls peering

SITE OF ANCIENT SCAFFOLD

HERE THE

EARL OF KILMARNOCK

AND

LORD BALMERINO

SUFFERED

18TH AUGUST 1746

12 Plaque marking the site of the last execution by beheading in London

out at anybody approaching. The entrance to St Olave's churchyard looks every bit as horrible, as can be seen in *figure 13*. The human skull is, of course, a recognised symbol in Christian iconography, but seldom, if ever, in this form. Immediately above the gate are three skulls, which make a bizarre enough sight, but it is the pillars on either side which really command the attention. As Dickens said, they are thrust through with spears. It looks for all the world as though these skulls have been skewered on spears and then set up as a warning. There is nothing like it anywhere else in London and it is an odd coincidence that it should stand here, so close to the site of so many beheadings. As we read above, Diodorus Siculus claimed that the Celts nailed heads up on the gate posts and this is just what these skulls look like.

While we are at Tower Hill, another site might repay a little attention. At the other end of Seething Lane from St Olave's is the church of All Hallows by the Tower. This is the oldest church in London and one of the oldest in the entire country. An unexpected consequence of bomb damage during the Second World War was the uncovering of a Saxon doorway from the original church which had been built over centuries ago. This is the only Saxon structure anywhere in London and has been constructed with the aid of Roman tiles. It pre-dates the nearby Tower of London by 400 years, having been built about 680. *Colour plate 8* shows this ancient doorway.

13 The gateway leading to St Olave's churchyard (*Tom Vivian*)

In the basement of this church is a Roman mosaic floor, proving that the Saxon church was built on the foundations of Roman building (*14*). Since this was the first church built in the city and knowing as we do of the custom of placing Christian places of worship on pagan sites, it could well be the case that the mosaic floor is from a temple rather than a house. Tower Hill was certainly a special place according to legend and it would not be at all surprising to find that a shrine and later a Romano-Celtic temple had been situated here. Whether or no, this church has a special connection with severed heads by virtue of the fact that the bodies of a number of those beheaded on Tower Hill were subsequently brought here before being buried.

These little stretches of Roman flooring found beneath old churches in London all look very similar. Beneath St Bride's in Fleet Street, Southwark Cathedral and also All Hallows by the Tower are identical pavements, consisting of small cubes of red tesserae. *Colour plate 10* shows this type of flooring from Southwark Cathedral and St Bride's church in Fleet Street. By an odd coincidence, exactly the same type of flooring was found at Silchester Forum, on the site of what is generally accepted to be the only Roman church discovered in this country. Intriguingly, the nearby parish church at Silchester is built over two Romano-Celtic temples. It is certainly possible that the finding of these Roman floors beneath three churches in London is a sign of continuity of use and that they were originally temples or shrines. In the case of St Bride's, this is almost certain; for Southwark Cathedral, likely; and for All Hallows, possible. Saxon settlement was almost entirely outside the old walled city of Londinium and so we are entitled to ask what it was about this particular spot which attracted a Saxon church builder of the seventh century.

The use to which the heads of the traitors executed at Tower Hill were put is also worth examining. Old London Bridge had many shops and houses along its length, rather like the present-day Ponte Vechio in Florence. At the Southwark end of the bridge, guarding the crossing to the walled City of London, was a gatehouse. It was here that the Keeper of the Heads had his official residence. His job was to make sure that the heads of executed men were properly displayed above the bridge's gatehouse. The ostensible idea was that these grim and gory relics would act as a deterrent to those minded to conspire against the monarch, but the whole practice had its roots in a far earlier era.

We know that the heads of enemies were put on show in this way by the Celts of Gaul. A monumental archway, the entrance to a temple, has been found near Marseille. It has niches for skulls. In this country, the skull of a youth was found near St Albans showed signs of having been fixed to a pole at the entrance to a temple or sanctuary. This too dated from the Iron Age.

The heads above the gateway on London Bridge would be making a powerful statement to everybody who crossed the bridge. They would remain there for years at a time; the largest number ever counted at one time was 34. In later years

14 Roman red tesserae flooring from All Hallows by the Tower (*with kind permission of All Hallows by the Tower*)

it became the custom to boil these heads in a mixture of various spices in order to discourage carrion birds from pecking them to pieces. They were sometimes coated with pitch for the same reason. Before this, however, there was a clear expectation that the flesh of the heads would, in fact, be eaten by the birds. The words of the death sentence imposed upon those guilty of treason make this quite clear. For those who were to be hanged, drawn and quartered, for instance, the death sentence ended with these words: 'And lastly his body to be quartered and the quarters set up in some high and eminent place, to the view and detestation of men, and to become a prey for the fowls of the air.' This has echoes of the excarnation of bodies which was practised in the distant past, where predators such as carrion birds would strip the flesh from a corpse which had been exposed.

Another way in which the custom of exposing severed heads above the bridge tied in with older traditions lies in the ultimate method of disposal. When the heads had been pecked to pieces and were unrecognisable, it was the duty of the Keeper of the Heads to remove the more disreputable looking ones and throw them into the Thames. Once again, this shows the continuation of an exceedingly ancient practice from one age to the next.

Viewing the heads on London Bridge was by way of being a Sunday afternoon entertainment for many poor people. It was roughly comparable to visiting Madame Tussauds waxworks today; a chance to see the faces of people one would never get to meet in real life. The newly installed head of a prominent person would always bring crowds out to admire it.

Southwark was not the only place in London where severed heads were to be seen. One of the points at which the City of Westminster ends and London begins was in Fleet Street. A gateway stood here from the fourteenth century onwards and it was felt that displaying the heads and other parts of executed traitors might perhaps also be a good idea here. The old gateway was demolished in the seventeenth century and Sir Christopher Wren, architect of St Paul's Cathedral, was commissioned to design a new one.

The gateway at Temple Bar, a minor masterpiece of baroque architecture, was unveiled in 1684. It might have been thought that after the Restoration, a more civilised attitude towards death and mutilation might prevail, but the new gateway was used almost immediately for the display of traitor's heads. In keeping with the modern times, miniature telescopes were hired out by enterprising shopkeepers at a halfpenny a time, so that people could view the heads more easily. Notable heads which were put on spikes here included that of the Duke of Monmouth, Charles II's illegitimate son. The heads of those executed following the 1745 rebellion in Scotland were also placed on Temple Bar. The last ever placed on a spike above Temple Bar was that of Lord Lovat, the last man beheaded in Britain. Incredibly, some of these heads were still there in 1772. A storm that year dislodged two of them, which then rolled a considerable distance down Fleet Street, causing a woman to faint of shock when one bumped into her feet. By

1878, traffic in Fleet Street was becoming hampered by the Temple Bar gateway and it was dismantled and stored in Hertfordshire. A few years ago it was brought back to the city and it is now in Paternoster Square. *Colour plate 11* shows Temple Bar today, standing in the shadow of St Paul's Cathedral.

That the cult of the severed head was still flourishing up until the sixteenth century or so is shown by the story of some German craftsmen who worked at the royal mint, which was at that time in the Tower of London. These men had been made ill by the fumes from the metalworking. Sometimes, copper is mixed with arsenic and this can be a hazard to health if the fumes are inhaled during casting or refining of the metal. A remedy was sought and the idea was mooted that they might be healed by drinking from vessels made from human skulls. This was a practice common among various ancient peoples. It was once thought that the strength and vitality of the dead man might be transferred to the living by drinking from the skull.

The Keeper of the Heads at London Bridge was approached and he agreed to allow several of the heads above the gatehouse to be utilised. These had the tops sawn off and were cleaned out thoroughly before being used as cups. The experiment was not an unalloyed success; some of the men recovered, while others died. That even 1500 years after the Roman invasion, such magical remedies should be tried, suggests that the cult of the severed heads must have had a strong grip upon the country at one time.

In modern, industrialised, western society, we have very clear ideas about the position and role of the dead. We might venerate our ancestors and tribal elders in theory, but we do not want to have them hovering round too much unless they are needed to bolster an argument or make us feel good about ourselves. Even then, it is their memory we invoke and not their physical presence. We have strong taboos around human remains; our culture demands that we keep them separate from us in their own well-defined geographical locations. The walls and railings which surround graveyards are psychological as well as physical barriers.

Where corpses and body parts are now on display in London, they have a gruesome novelty value. We stare not with reverence and respect, but in horrified fascination. Several museums in London have corpses on display and, for most people, there is something distinctly creepy about them. The British Museum has a desiccated Egyptian corpse, with traces of hair still remaining on his scalp. His stone sarcophagus always has a crowd around it, frequently consisting of young people saying 'Oh, yuk!' In the University of London, the stuffed corpse of Jeremy Bentham, the famous Utilitarian philosopher, is seated in a glass case. His head has been replaced by a waxwork and the usual emotion evinced by those who come to see him is nervous amusement (at one time, Bentham's severed and preserved head was positioned between his feet; this has now been removed). We wish for the dead to be physically removed from our presence as soon as possible after death and definitely do not wish to hear from them or see them again once the funeral is over.

As well as taboos about corpses and skeletons, there is still a fairly strong cultural prohibition in Britain against contacting, conversing with or indeed having
any communication at all with the dead. We neither summon up their spirits, nor
do we wish them to appear before us uninvited. These apparitions are what we
call ghosts and they are almost universally unwelcome.

The concept of a proper and codified separation between the physical worlds
of the living and the dead was introduced to this country by the Romans. They
had laws which forbade the burying of corpses within a walled city. This was
in contrast to those living in Britain at the time of the Roman invasion. For
them, corpses had no horrors and were an accepted part of their everyday life.
The Roman prohibition on contact with the dead was later endorsed by the
Christians. The ban on contacting the dead in trances or through magic, though,
did not arrive in this country until Christian missionaries began proselytising and
is firmly rooted in the Judeo-Christian tradition. The Bible forbids absolutely the
conjuring up of the dead.

Many, perhaps most, early cultures had a relaxed and welcoming attitude
towards the dead. Their physical presence, in the form of skulls and other bones,
was acceptable and so were attempts to communicate with them via trances or
other methods. When the Hebrews conquered the land of Canaan in around
1500 BC, they found a typical example of such a culture. It must have been a
bit like ancient Britain. There were altars on hilltops, worship of the sacred bull,
free communication with the dead and a cult of the severed head flourishing
in at least one city. By an odd coincidence, there were also face pots of the sort
which became popular among the Romanised Celts in Londinium. As a way of
distinguishing themselves from every other nation of that time, a set of taboos
and prohibitions were imposed upon the Jews by their wise men and prophets.
These related to every aspect of life, from eating prawns to collecting firewood
on the seventh day of the week. Very early on in the Bible, in Deuteronomy, the
Hebrews were told: 'Don't let your people practice divination or look for omens
and don't let them consult the spirits of the dead.' The death penalty was pre-
scribed for those who tried to communicate with the dead.

At the same time, a code of taboos were put into place around corpses, which
were to be regarded as ritually unclean and had to be disposed of as swiftly as possible. To the other peoples of the Middle East at that time, the Hebrew attitude
to the dead was as weird as the fact that they would not eat pigs or worship the
images of bulls. Christianity adopted these prohibitions wholesale and this in turn
led to the abolition of many traditional religious practices in Europe.

To see how the early inhabitants of London viewed the dead members of their
community, it will be necessary to look first at the practices of those in other
parts of Europe who first lived in urban communities. At Catal Huyuk, family
members who died had their bones interred beneath the floors of the houses.
Specifically, they were embedded in the plaster of the sleeping areas. It seems that

the citizens of this Stone Age town were extremely involved with the dead. At Lepenski Vir too, corpses were buried beneath the floors of the homes. In Jericho, an even more intimate relationship was maintained with dead relatives, with their skulls being kept on the Neolithic equivalent of the mantelpiece.

The practices at Catal Huyk, Lepenski Vir and Jericho indicate strongly that from the very beginning of humanity's settled lifestyle, both religion and the care of the dead were of paramount importance. It might be said that a cult of the dead was the norm for both town dwellers and farmers from the first days of the agricultural revolution which ushered in the Neolithic period. Even before this, human skeletons are found in caves in which people were living for centuries. When members of a group like this died, their bodies were buried beneath the living area.

What do we mean by the expression 'a cult of the dead'? In our society, the dead play a very little role. There are some customs which are pretty generally observed as far as dead people are concerned: it is considered to be in poor taste to speak ill of the dead. The more recently the person has died, the less apt are people to say anything unpleasant about him. To us, this seems like a social rule and really no more than common courtesy, but the Latin saying, *De mortuis nil nisi bonum*, speak only well of the dead, has deep roots in the past. Apart from speaking no ill of the dead, what else must we do or refrain from doing? We lay our dead friends and relatives to rest with appropriate rites, playing music and praising their memory. Sometimes we bring them gifts of flowers on the anniversary of their death and ensure that they will not be forgotten, by placing a stone slab above their last resting place to commemorate their name. We tell our children about the wise sayings and good deeds of their great-grandparents. Perhaps we might take them to visit their dead ancestors at a cemetery once in a while.

Whatever our religion, we think that the spirits of the dead have left the earth and have no further concern with it. They cease from the moment they stop breathing to be members of our society. Any courtesies done to them or respect given is a favour which we are granting. They have gone and we remain. When we encounter corpses or body parts, we feel that there is something wrong and unnatural. This is so ingrained these days that it seems like a natural and healthy reaction. Similarly, if we believe that the spirits of the dead are abroad, we feel profoundly uneasy. Few people wish to be haunted.

The situation in Britain was once quite different. The dead were thought of as full members of the community and their views and opinions were at least as important as anybody else's. More so in some ways, because the dead could cause a lot of harm if they became angry or vengeful. The amount of damage liable to be wrought by an aggrieved living man could be gauged pretty accurately, but nobody knew for sure what an angry dead person might be capable of. Causing cows to stop producing milk, lightning to strike a barn, illness to carry off a child – there was no limit at all to the powers of the dead. For this reason, they must be honoured, treated with respect and properly provided for so that they would not become discontented with their lot and seek to walk the earth again.

Not only was it wise to pay attention to the dead because of the injury which they might cause if treated disrespectfully; there was another reason that it was not wise to disregard them. This was because the dead were now resident in the world of the gods and spirits. They might be rubbing shoulders with the cleverest people who had ever lived and also consorting regularly with various deities. Their views and opinions were sure to be more important and far better informed now than when they were alive. This was why the summoning up of the dead in different ways was undertaken on a regular basis in the ancient world; the dead had plenty to say that was worth hearing.

The desire to mark the interment of the dead with special rites and the supposed need to provide them with the things that they would need in the next world are universal in the ancient world. Often, those honoured in this way would be only the royalty or priesthood. In ancient Britain, a situation evolved where the whole of society was geared to producing material wealth for both the gods and the dead. Not only material wealth in the form of produced objects, but also any surplus labour was expended on projects for the benefit of the dead. Few traces remain in England of domestic architecture before the Roman invasion – half a dozen huts in Cornwall and that is about it. But scattered everywhere are barrows, earthworks and stone monuments. All that remains of prehistoric society in most of the country is that which related to the worship of gods or reverence for ancestors. It is an extraordinary situation.

A future archaeologist conducting a dig on a twenty-first-century site would find immeasurably more concerning the living and their needs than he would religious shrines or monuments for the dead. Consider any neighbourhood in the country. A scattering of churches and mosques, the occasional graveyard, but beyond that, every structure has been built with the living in mind. From the Neolithic and Bronze Age, precisely the opposite is true. The only things which remain visible are those which were involved with either religious observance or the needs of the dead. Barrows, menhirs, causewayed enclosures, henges, cursuses; these all shaped the landscape in which they community lived, but were of no benefit to the living at all.

Most of the prehistoric remains which are known in the London area are those associated with the dead. In Chapter 2 we examined the causewayed enclosure which is now buried beneath the M25 motorway. We also looked at the Shepperton henge. Both these sites were intimately associated with both the living and the dead. There was certainly feasting, and also deposition of food in specially dug holes or shafts. These ritual shafts were a way of sending goods to the world of the dead, rather like the depositions in the Thames and other watery locations. It is likely that the causewayed enclosure was sometimes used as a mortuary, where decomposing corpses would be exposed for insects and birds to remove the flesh. The same place was also used for communal gatherings and feasts.

So different is this lifestyle from out own, that we cannot really grasp what was happening at places like Yeoveny Lodge or Shepperton henge. Imagine for a moment a clearing by the local river where rotting corpses of family members were left lying around for months. This would not strike many of us today as the ideal spot for a picnic and yet that is exactly what took place. The remains of feasts have been found in the ditches, all jumbled up with unwanted human bones. Burials took place at these sites as well. It is plain that those who ate there were both enjoying a day out and also visiting the dead in the most intimate fashion imaginable: sitting for their picnic among the decomposing remains of friends and family.

Long after Christianity had become universal in this country, traces of the cult of the dead were still to be widely found. Passed down by oral tradition, however, they became distorted and misunderstood, although still an integral part of the lives of ordinary people, especially those who lived in rural areas. One thing to bear in mind is that the dead were never seen as being wholly benevolent. They might aid a man or they might just as easily hinder him. It was necessary to court them and furnish them with what they required if one hoped to enlist their assistance. These characteristics were remembered for thousands of years after the explicit belief system to which they belonged had passed away. They account for much of our current rituals and traditions for disposing of and honouring the dead.

One other piece of religious observance seems to have permeated the lives of communities in this country before the coming of the Romans. This is the veneration given to the sun and the heavens in general. There is good reason to suppose that prehistoric people in Europe worshipped the sun. We can certainly assert with confidence that they followed keenly the movement of the sun across the heavens, not just from day to day but across the course of the year and even over periods of decades. There is evidence for this in the London area. Because modern London has obliterated all traces of many of the subtler and more elusive signs of early habitation and worship, we must look beyond the built-up areas for signs of anything of this sort.

A great deal has been written about the alignment of megalithic tombs and monuments to various risings of the sun – midwinter, summer solstice and so on. Stonehenge has been particularly studied in this respect and many extravagant claims made for the astronomical data need to construct this circular array of stones on Salisbury common. Stonehenge was not, of course, the only henge monument in Britain. It is without doubt the most striking and impressive, but other circular ditches of this kind are to be found scattered around the country, including the Shepperton henge.

Not far from this henge was an Iron Age village known as Caesar's Camp, which now lies under a runway at Heathrow. This consisted of a cluster of round-houses and also a curious rectangular building which has been interpreted as being a temple or shrine. It is an inexplicable fact that rectangular houses or huts were all but unknown in Britain until the Roman invasion. Long barrows, such as West Kennet on Salisbury Plain, are rectangular, but not domestic architecture. There are several theories as to why this should be, but any building which violates this apparent rule is generally supposed to be a place of worship. Caesar's Camp is remarkable not merely for its shrine, but also for the fact that the doorways of all the huts, like the entrance to the henge at Shepperton, face the rising sun on midsummer's day. This can scarcely have been chance.

Alignments of this kind are seen in places like the tomb at Newgrange in Ireland, where the sun at the winter solstice shines straight down a passageway and into the heart of the tomb. This sort of thing suggests a long history not only of observation, but of the recording of these observations. How these records were kept, we have no idea. From time to time pieces of wood or ivory are found from the Stone Age with scratches and other marks, rather like tally sticks. It has been thought that these might have formed part of a system for keeping track of the phases of the moon and apparent movement of the sun along the horizon as the year progresses.

What is beyond all doubt is that the Druids, inheritors and keepers of a tradition far older than their own Iron Age culture, were keenly interested in the movements of the sun, moon and stars. Classical writers told of their fascination with the heavens and some of the observations which they made. Julius Caesar wrote that the Druids were concerned with 'the stars and their movements, the size of the cosmos and the earth, the world of nature, the powers of deities'. The Druids were aware of the Metonic Cycle, which argues a fair degree of sophistication in their measurements and recordkeeping. This cycle, in which the orbits of the earth and moon and earth relative to the sun synchronise, can be used to predict lunar eclipses.

It is uncommon in the Greater London area for an entire village to be excavated systematically; usually only one or two huts are examined. Looking at Caesar's Camp and the Shepperton henge, makes it seem likely that this kind of alignment to important movements of the sun might have been the rule rather than the exception, at least in the Thames valley area.

Observations of this sort and predictions about the movements of heavenly bodies would have been useful from both a religious and practical point of view. Knowing when the days were getting shorter or longer, and particularly the equinoxes in September and March, would have been helpful in deciding when to sow and reap crops. It would also have been helpful in fixing the times of festivals and celebrations. As the days shortened after the autumn equinox, there must have been a feeling of uneasiness on the part of many primitive people. Suppose that the days continued to get shorter like this? Suppose that the days just got shorter and shorter until they dwindled away to nothing and the earth was cloaked in darkness? This is, of course, the origin of our Christmas festival. This solstice was in many cultures a time for celebration and feasting. At both Stonehenge and

Newgrange, the winter solstice could be calculated precisely. At Newgrange the sunrise on that day was the key moment; at Stonehenge it was sunset.

The winter solstice falls on 21 or 22 December. It took a few days after that point when it was clear that the sun had reversed its movement along the horizon and the days were indeed becoming longer. It is at this point, three or four days after the solstice, that we celebrate Christmas as our ancestors celebrated at the same time of year, by feasting and drunkenness.

Observation of the heavens would have been vital even before the advent of agriculture. Wandering bands of hunters would have used the stars to navigate, especially those like Polaris, the Pole Star, which indicated true north. The shortening or lengthening of the days and seasonal change in the constellations would also have been important in predicting the migration of the herds of the animals upon which Palaeolithic communities depended for their food.

7

Cultural Diffusion and the Preservation of Myth

It will not have escaped the reader's notice that many of the things which have been discussed so far are common throughout history in widely separated parts of the world. Casting valuable metal objects into a body of water has, of course, parallels with the legend of El Dorado.

In Columbia is an extinct volcano whose crater is full of water. It is called Lake Guatavita. It was the custom before the coming of the Spanish for the local king to be smeared with resin and then coated with powdered gold. He and his retinue set out to the middle of the lake in a ceremonial raft. The king would then bathe in the lake, the gold dust being washed from his naked body and sinking to the bottom of the lake. At the same time, his attendants cast ornaments made of solid gold into the dark waters of Guatavita. This was the basis for the legend of El Dorado: the Golden Man. If gold had been more plentiful than copper and tin in this country, there can be little doubt that the ancient Britons would have followed the same kind of ritual, rather than merely hurling bronze swords and flint axes into the Thames.

These customs are identical. Gold was plentiful in that part of South America and so it was the metal used to make offerings to the gods. In Britain, copper was the metal most often used. The same principle is at work: making objects from metal and then dropping them beyond reach into the depths of a river or lake. It is quite likely that both the ceremonies at Lake Guatavita and those in London had a common origin. After all, the Amerindians of South America came from the Eurasian landmass, presumably carrying with them in addition to their spears and cooking pots, their cultural heritage and religious beliefs.

As a matter of fact, something remarkably similar to the ritual depositions of gold made at Guatavita did happen in this country, although not in London. A small, clearly delineated area in Norfolk has yielded many gold torcs, buried as hoards over 2000 years ago. The torc, like a crown, had complex symbolism,

1a The stone coffin at Southwark Cathedral (*Tom Vivian, with kind permission of Southwark Cathedral*)

1b The head of the coffin and the visible portion of first-century Roman road at Southwark Cathedral (*Tom Vivian, with kind permission of Southwark Cathedral*)

2 Roman Londinium (*Tom Vivian, with kind permission of All Hallows by the Tower*)

3 The Roman temple of Mithras on the bank of the Walbrook river (*Tom Vivian*)

4 The Roman temple of Mithras on the bank of the Walbrook river

5 The site of Merlin's Cave at the top of Pentonville Road, Islington (*Tom Vivian*)

7 Reconstruction of Romano-Celtic temple at Greenwich (*with kind permission of Channel 4 and the* Time Team)

8 The Saxon archway at All Hallows by the Tower (*Tom Vivian, with kind permission of All Hallows by the Tower*)

9 The Roman pavement at All Hallows by the Tower, one of the most perfectly preserved tessellated Roman pavements in the City of London (*Tom Vivian, with kind permission of All Hallows by the Tower*)

10 The small portion of Roman pavement preserved in Southwark Cathedral (*Tom Vivian, with kind permission of Southwark Cathedral*)

11 Temple Bar Gateway

12 The Bronze Age round barrows at Greenwich. It is impossible to distinguish between them and the later Saxon barrows

13 The Walbrook flowing
through Londinium and out
into the Thames (*with kind
permission of All Hallows by the
Tower*)

14 The spire of St Bride's in
Fleet Street, model for wedding
cakes for over 200 years
(*Tom Vivian*)

15 The statue of a hunter god recovered in 1977 from the well beneath Southwark Cathedral (*Tom Vivian, with kind permission of Southwark Cathedral*)

16 Southwark Cathedral

17 A curious gallery of historic artefacts in the crypt beneath St Bride's church
(*Tom Vivian, with kind permission of St Bride's*)

18a, b & c A selection of architectural fragments, revealing earlier phases of Southwark Cathedral (*with kind permission of Southwark Cathedral*)

19a Cast of a Roman tombstone found in Moorgate in 1911. The inscription reads 'To Marcus Aurelius Eucarpus, most devoted Son, aged 15 years 6 months. Set up by his mother, Aurelia Eucarpia' (*with kind permission of All Hallows by the Tower*)

19b Cast of a Roman tombstone found in Doodman's Fields in 1787. The original is in the British Museum. The inscription reads 'In memory of Flavius Agricola, soldier of the Sixth Legion, "The Victorious". He lived 42 years, 10 days. Albua Faustina set this up to her incomparable husband' (*with kind permission of All Hallows by the Tower*)

19c Cast of a Roman tombstone found on Tower Hill in 1852. The original is in the British Museum. The inscription reads 'Allus Alfidius Olussa of the Pomptine Tribe, a native of Atiena. He lived 70 years. His heirs erected this in accordance with his will. He lies here' (*with kind permission of All Hallows by the Tower*)

including perhaps nobility and deity. Images of gods from the Celtic era often show them wearing torcs. Perhaps this burying of golden torcs was, like the ceremonies in Columbia, some rite practised by the royalty of this country.

At one time, and not very long ago at that, new cultures, technology and languages in ancient times were thought of as having been spread by the edge of the sword. The Indo-Europeans marched relentlessly from their ancestral homelands, slashing and burning as they went. They had the horse and the wheel, and the technologically inferior civilisations in their way were ruthlessly conquered, before being massacred or subjugated. The history of Europe and Britain was seen as a succession of assaults from the east; starting with the invasion of the Cro-Magnons and continuing through to the savage incursions of Iron Age warriors into the British Isles. This is no longer the generally accepted view of European prehistory.

There is solid scientific reason to doubt that physical incursions of new populations took place on a large scale before the Roman invasion. In 1996, mitochondrial DNA was extracted and sequenced from the tooth of a skeleton found in Cheddar Gorge at the beginning of the last century. This skeleton was of a man who died over 9000 years ago, at a time before the introduction of agriculture to Britain. Twenty residents of the area agreed to have their own mitochondrial DNA tested. Exact matches were found in two children and a partial match in another person. These people were actually related to the 9000-year-old man found in a cave in the gorge. Specifically, this meant that both they and the man from Cheddar Gorge had a common female ancestor.

This was seen by some as the final nail in the coffin of the theory that agriculture and other cultural developments had been brought to this country by newcomers from Europe or the Middle East, who replaced the existing population of this country. If this had happened, then it is unlikely that any relatives of Cheddar Gorge man would still be living in the same vicinity almost 10,000 years later.

Ten thousand years ago, the people of Europe lived in tribes who wandered across the continent in search of food. These people might winter somewhere or linger in some lush spot for a few months in the summer, but they were essentially nomadic, moving restlessly from one place to another. Farming, by which is meant the cultivation of crops and the keeping of useful domesticated animals, requires a fixed and immobile lifestyle. One sows the seed and must still be in the same place when harvest time arrives in the autumn. Agriculture began in several different locations independently throughout the world, but the agricultural revolution in Europe began in the Middle East and spread to Europe 9000 years ago, via Greece.

The use of metals also started in the Middle East and reached Europe in the same way. These new lifestyles took thousands of years to diffuse in the direction of Britain. New people and new ideas moved along coasts and river valleys, slowed by mountain ranges, thick forests and the sea. In geographically isolated places, old ways of doing things and old ideas could be bypassed by whatever cultural revolution was sweeping through the more accessible parts of a region. Hunting communities could continue their lifestyle and follow their traditional practices, despite the fact that all around them permanent settlements were being formed.

Other cultural movements which originated in the Middle East and then travelled to Europe were writing and, much later, monotheism. Writing spread first to Greece and from there to Italy. The Roman Empire then introduced the concept of literacy to the rest of Europe. The monotheistic faith of Christianity also flourished in the countries occupied by Rome. These were essentially movements of ideas rather than people.

How does all this relate to London? During the 1930s, when the Ford factory was being built at Dagenham, in East London, a strangely shaped bit of wood turned up in the mud that was being cleared from the site. Nineteen inches long, it was a grotesque idol, such as one might expect to find being worshipped by a primitive tribe on some remote Pacific island. The weirdly proportioned human figure was carved from Scots Pine and carbon dating after the Second World War showed it to be 4500 years old, the oldest representation of a human figure known in this country.

The Dagenham idol, as it became known, was buried next to the skeleton of a deer; it is not unreasonable to suppose that it was connected in some way with the cult of hunting and the stag. The area was marshland and this was a ritual deposit of some kind. There were a couple of peculiarities about this crudely carved, doll-like piece of wood which shed light upon several of the ideas at which we have been looking. Most notably, although one of the eyes was a deeply gouged, circular hole, the other was merely a shallow indentation. It seemed as though this idol had been intended to represent somebody with only one eye. The other curious feature was that instead of recognisable genitals, the figure had a large hole in its groin. This was thought to have been for the purpose of fitting it with an enormous phallus, which would be plugged into the hole.

Assuming that the idol was supposed to depict some god, the obvious candidate must be Odin, the mightiest god of the Norsemen, known also to the Saxons as Woden. Several representations of this god are known from Europe and these have holes just like the Dagenham idol for penises to be attached. There is a slight difficulty with all this, though, because Odin or Woden was a god of the Germanic tribes or the Scandinavians in the first few centuries of the Christian era. The Dagenham idol predates the Norse mythology by some 3000 years. What was a one-eyed god doing in the Thames marshes thousands of years before anybody hears anything at all of the one-eyed Odin of the Norsemen?

Germany and Scandinavia were, like Britain itself, a little off the beaten track from mainstream European culture. Customs and ideas which had been superseded in the rest of Europe were able to survive in such regions. Neither Germany nor Scandinavia formed part of the Roman Empire and so escaped the effects not only of the introduction of Christianity, but also of the Roman lifestyle, which

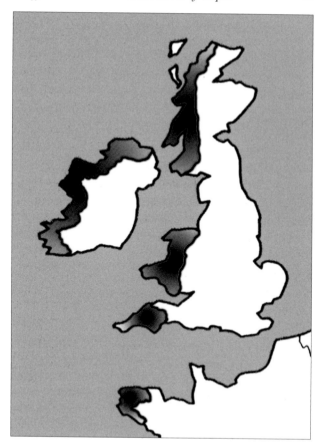

15 The Celtic Fringe

at that time represented the most advanced thinking in Europe on most matters. Perhaps an analogy might make the matter a little clearer.

The Celtic Fringe refers to that part of Atlantic Europe where the Celtic language, customs, traditions and religious beliefs lingered on after the rest of Europe had become Latinised. Cornwall, Wales, Ireland, Scotland and the western tip of Brittany in France comprise this region. *Figure 15* illustrates this and makes it clear that the so-called Celtic Fringe is, geographically, the furthest from mainland Europe. A version of the old Celtic language is spoken to this day by hundreds of thousands of people in Wales, as well as some thousands in Scotland and Ireland and a few in Brittany. As well as the language, customs which died out decades or centuries ago in the rest of Western Europe are still practised in these places.

The reverence for wells and their treatment as places to strike bargains with the gods is a good example of a custom which is still practised in parts of the Celtic Fringe, long after it has vanished from the rest of this country. At some wells in Ireland, pieces of cloth and offerings are placed. In Scotland, also in the Celtic Fringe, such places are known as Cloti Wells.

The position in the British Isles as a whole was much the same 2000 years ago as the Celtic Fringe. Old customs and beliefs were to be found here which had perhaps been all but forgotten in mainland Europe. Not in Scandinavia, though, which was separated by the sea from the mainstream of European culture, nor in a few areas on the periphery of the continent. This is why the Vikings and Saxons from Denmark and North Germany found that their belief system had much in common with that of the British. The first people in this country had come here in waves from the end of the last ice age. They migrated across the plain of the North Sea, which was at that time dry land. With them from Europe they brought the mythology and beliefs of the Old Stone Age hunters and gatherers who formed the only communities on that continent for hundreds of thousands of years. This lifestyle, where the success at the hunt was a matter not of prestige but of life and death, cannot fail to have left its mark upon those thousands of generations who pursued it. The image of the horned or tusked beasts which they hunted must have left an indelible imprint upon the unconscious mind of these tribes. They might have pursued and killed the mammoth and later the wild stag, boar and aurochs, but at that the same time they were profoundly grateful to the animals for all that they gave them: the leather and fur, horn and bone, meat and fuel to cook it by. The men and women of the tribe would imitate the stag, dress up in its skin, enact a successful hunt as a form of sympathetic magic. The prevalence of antlers found in graves suggests that the stag or horned beast in general was a universal totem.

Figure 16 shows Europe looked at from the same perspective which produced the Celtic Fringe. Instead of Celtic culture surviving on the very outskirts of Atlantic Europe, we have pre-Celtic and in some cases, perhaps even pre-Indo-European myths and traditions which have remained unchanged on the edge of Europe.

Much of Europe and South Asia shares a common heritage of language and myth. There are marked similarities between the gods and goddesses of ancient Greece and Rome and also of Rome and India. Their languages also have many similarities – far too many to be coincidental. It was first noticed in the late eighteenth century that Sanskrit, a very ancient language of India, is similar in form and grammatical structure to both Latin and Greek. Etymological analysis shows that both had a common ancestor.

There is still furious debate among scholars as to the exact sequence of events which led both India and Western Europe to have languages with a common origin. Most agree that about 8000 years ago a tribe speaking what has become known as proto Indo-European left their homelands somewhere near the Black Sea and spread out towards Europe and India, taking with them not only their language, but the rest of their culture, including their religious beliefs. This was probably not a wave of conquest, more small groups moving outward and settling in various fertile plains and river valleys. After a few centuries, the movement across Europe would have been not a physical one of settlers and immigrants, but

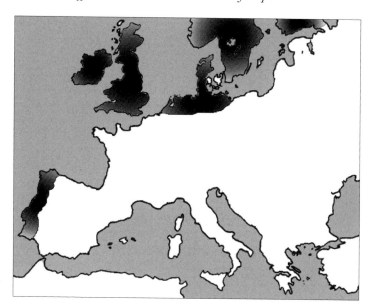

16 The
pre-Celtic or
Indo-European
'Fringe'

more a transfer of ideas and language. By about 1000 BC, much of Europe was speaking versions of the Indo-European language and had perhaps adopted their mythology, but not Britain which was insulated by the sea from many cultural developments on the mainland.

The agricultural revolution of the Neolithic Age though had reached Britain and the society there had changed in the millennia before Christ into an agrarian rather than a hunter-gatherer society. As this had gradually happened, hunting and all that had been associated with it became a memory; a memory which became first sentimentalised and then sanctified. For the comfortable farmers, the idea of men living entirely by what they could catch on any given day must have seemed like a mythic age of heroism.

It might be an idea to say a few words here about the meaning of the word myth. We use the word interchangeably these days with 'lie' and 'falsehood'. This is a shame, because myths are not really lies at all. Often they express deep truths in a poetic form. The myth of Cinderella, for instance, which occurs throughout many cultures, has something to tell us about blended families and the role of step-parents. The latest studies in sociology confirm that the wicked step-parent is far from being an imaginary ogre. A nation's myths can tell us a lot about the people who have created and cherished them. It is worth noting that many of Britain's myths include resistance to invasion; not necessarily in the form of armed men, but certainly in the sense of the country being swamped by newcomers. This enduring mythic narrative is still going strong, of course. One only needs to glance at any newspaper to see concerns over the influx of foreigners with new languages and unfamiliar customs. The whole idea of waves of strangers disrupting our traditional way of life has been a stock image here for at least 5000 years. Caractacus, Boudica, King Arthur, Hereward the Wake, Robin Hood, Churchill, the Battle of Britain, influxes of foreign immigrants – all these say something about how the British see themselves and their place in the world. For our purposes here, we shall adopt a definition of myth as a recurring narrative which expresses the hopes and fears of a particular group.

Returning to London, it has been observed that when the Saxons came to this country in great numbers after the fall of the Roman Empire and the withdrawal of the legions that were protecting this island from invasion, they seemed to have found that they had quite a bit in common with those already living in the British Isles. There were skirmishes and territorial disputes, such things were inevitable, but there was also intermarriage, with Briton and Saxon rubbing along together. This might well have been because the Saxons and Angles themselves had come from parts of Europe where, just as in Britain, older traditions might have been preserved. They had more in common with the British than they would with say the Italians or Greeks.

We have reason to believe this, because many artefacts have been recovered from bogs in Denmark and other parts of Northern Europe. The Gundestrap, Cauldron, for instance had been dismantled and placed in a Danish bog, obviously as an offering. Humans too had been sacrificed in bogs and this is also seen both in Denmark and this country. These are traditions which flourished on the fringe of civilised Europe, rather than in the heartland which was dominated by Greco-Roman *mores*.

At Greenwich, the Saxons began burying their dead in round barrows on the site of the old Bronze Age cemetery. Today, one cannot tell which of the round barrows are Saxon and which date from the Bronze Age. *Colour plate 12* shows a round barrow at Greenwich; impossible to tell whether from the Bronze Age or a later Saxon burial. In Kingston-upon-Thames the practice of ritual deposition was resumed. In 1989 a site at Eden Street in Kingston was explored. Masses of coins from the fourth century were found in an old river bed, along with a great deal of copper alloy jewellery. Except for the fact that they were a thousand years more recent, these depositions could have been from the Iron Age. This was in fact an Iron Age ritual site and was in some way recognised by the Saxons when they arrived. This strongly suggests that whatever the derivation of the religious practices in this island, the Saxons felt quite at home with them and were content to use the existing cemeteries and ritual sites which they found when they moved here.

The Dagenham idol indicates that a one-eyed god who might have been a prototype for Odin or Woden was familiar to the people living near London 3000 years before the Anglo-Saxons came here. The Anglo-Saxon kings claimed that they were descended from Woden, another name for Odin. Both Odin and Woden are famous for leading the Wild Hunt. This mythological event was a confused mêlée of ghostly men, dogs and horses which swept across the country-side, and sometimes also the sky, in pursuit of a stag. This image of hunting deer would have struck a deep resonance with the Romanised Celts who were living here before the Saxons. Perhaps it was a garbled folk memory of the real hunts which were once vital to the survival of the tribes who lived here before the introduction of farming.

In Germany and Scandinavia, the Wild Hunt was associated with Woden, but in this country it was thought to be led by, among others, Hereward the Wake and Herne the Hunter. Hereward, the resister against the foreign invader, we have seen as a stock figure of British folklore. We have not yet looked at Herne, one of the most intriguing characters from British mythology. Shakespeare was familiar with the legend of Herne the Hunter, who haunted the Thames near Windsor. In *The Merry Wives of Windsor*, Shakespeare wrote:

Sometime a keeper here in Windsor Forest,
Doth all the winter-time, at still midnight,
Walk round about an oak, with great ragg'd horns;
And there he blasts the tree, and takes the cattle,
And makes milch-kine yield blood, and shakes a chain
In a most hideous and dreadful manner.
You have heard of such a spirit, and well you know
The superstitious idle-headed eld
Receiv'd, and did deliver to our age,
This tale of Herne the Hunter for a truth.

'With great ragged horns': here is the origin of Herne, leader of the Wild Hunt. Herne has antlers sprouting from his head; he is cognate with both Cernunnos and the sorcerer of Trois Frères. The image of Herne the Hunter, the mighty human hunter with his antlered head pursuing the stag across the countryside, is the ultimate identification of the hunter with his prey. Here, the hunter has in some sense become the prey, taken on its physical characteristics. Woden or Hereward, Herne or Cernunnos, this is the same archetypal figure. The Saxons and later the Vikings would have had no difficulty at all in adapting to the British myth system. Both had a common heritage which pre-dated even the Indo-Europeans, a folk memory of the group hunt, where a wild and confused mass of men and dogs chased and killed stags. This noisy and chaotic enterprise would have been preceded historically by rituals and dances in which those who would take part in the hunt enacted a successful outcome with some placing antlers on their heads and mimicking the death of the quarry.

A relic of the rituals observed regarding Odin is still practised in this country, although its pagan origins have long been forgotten. Once again, it involves ant-lers and horns. Odin was chief of the Norse gods and one of his fellow gods was

Thor, god of war. Odin rode on a magic horse called Sleipnir, but Thor rode in a chariot drawn by two goats. Thor, of course, carried a hammer and is perhaps identical with the Celtic god Sucellos, who also carried a hammer and shared many of Thor's traits. Odin and Thor have been combined into one mighty mythic figure of present-day Britain who combines notable features of both gods.

In Scandinavia, the few days after the winter solstice were known as Yule, from which we derive the term Yuletide. This festival was sacred to both Odin and Thor. Children used to put straw in their shoes when they went to bed at night. They did this to provide food for Odin's horse and the god would sometimes replace the straw with sweets or other little gifts. Odin himself had the appearance when he visited the earth of an old man with a long white beard and a hood or floppy hat pulled over his face. If we combine these attributes with those of Thor, who rode in a vehicle drawn by horned animals, we see the hooded figure of Father Christmas in a sleigh, pulled along by reindeer. Even today, some children in Britain leave out carrots for the reindeer and a glass of beer and a mince pie for Father Christmas. This simple, childish custom has its roots in the rituals performed by the Vikings and Saxons, based upon mythic archetypes which were thousands of years old.

Other customs which the Saxons would already know when they came to Britain entailed the sacrifice of horned and tusked animals, such as deer, boars and cattle. We saw Pope Gregory inveighing against this shortly after the fall of the Roman Empire and there is little doubt that it was the Saxons and Angles whom he had in mind. When the barrow at Sutton Hoo in Suffolk was opened, it seemed almost identical to some of the Bronze Age tombs in Europe. All the worldly goods of the chieftain were here, even down to his boat. It will come as no surprise to learn that red deer were also sacrificed as part of the burial rites at Sutton Hoo.

A Greek myth which might repay close examination when we are thinking about hunting and the powerful identification of the hunter with his prey is that of Actaeon and Artemis. Although this is a Greek myth, the subject itself must be very ancient, far pre-dating Hellenic civilisation. Artemis is the same hunting goddess known to the Romans as Diana.

There was once a mighty hunter called Actaeon. He was the greatest hunter who had ever lived and his palace was decorated with trophies of the animals which he had slain. His chief delight was in hunting the stag. Even his furniture was made of antlers and tusks. He had a pack of fierce and cunning hounds. Each had its own special characteristic: one was old and ruthless, another extremely fast, a third very clever and so on. One of these dogs was half wolf, which made him especially ferocious.

One day Actaeon was out hunting with his dogs. He wandered into a part of the wild country where he had never been before. Dismounting from his horse, he went alone towards a pool where he could hear the voices of young women, shouting and laughing. He crept up, hiding behind some trees and shrubs and found himself witnessing something which no mortal man had ever seen before. Artemis, goddess of hunting and the moon, was bathing with her a group of nymphs. They were naked and Actaeon could not tear his eyes away from Artemis, who was the most beautiful young woman he had ever seen. Artemis was perpetually virgin and chaste; no man had ever seen her naked.

The goddess was suddenly aware of Actaeon hiding in the bushes and she was furious that anybody, man or god, should dare to spy on her in this way. She looked at Actaeon, who found himself unable to speak. Before he knew what was happening, Actaeon felt a terrible pain in his temples and collapsed to the ground in agony. His limbs were stretching and twisting and the pain in his head grew unbearable. The maidens had vanished and he was alone by the waterfall. He crawled over to the pool and looked down into it. To his amazement, he saw a stag peering back at him. As he shook his head in amazement, the stag shook his head. Then Actaeon realised what had happened. Artemis had punished him for seeing her nakedness. She had turned him into a stag.

In the distance he heard a terrible sound; it was the baying of a pack of hounds – his own hounds. Those dogs had never once let their prey escape from them. They could follow a scent for the whole day and long into the night. No animal had ever been able to outrun them. Actaeon leaped up and ran for his life. The hounds had caught the scent of a deer and were soon streaming across the countryside in pursuit. The end was never in doubt and, before the night was out, Actaeon had been torn to pieces by his own hunting dogs.

This mythic image, of the hunter who identifies so closely with his quarry that he actually becomes the very animal he pursues, is one of the primal archetypes of man's past. Here is the sorcerer of Trois Frères, Herne the Hunter, Cernunnos, the dancers of Abbots Bromley: the humans assuming the identity of the prey until they are one with him. The horned beast is both the sacrifice and the totem of the tribe: the hunted, but also the hunter.

There are other basic mythic archetypes embedded within this narrative. The perpetually virgin goddess, who in this case is Artemis, could also be the Virgin Mary; and the Peeping Tom who gazed upon Lady Godiva and was struck blind in punishment. The more one delves into this story, the richer it becomes.

There are so many similarities between the myth systems of Greece, Rome, Celtic Britain, India and a hundred other cultures that it is beyond reason that they all should have sprung up independently. Take the votive offerings which have been such a recurring theme in London's history, beginning many thousands of years ago. The idea behind these offerings in exchange for favours from the deity is one of contract. It is a purely business arrangement with the god or goddess. The god performs a service for the worshipper, who in return leaves goods or money in payment. This view of religious duty was at once recognised by the Romans when they came here as being a quite fit and proper way of carrying on. It was, after all, their own system. They provided worship and the outwards rituals and forms of respect, and in return their gods protected them and caused their ventures to prosper. If an enterprise failed, it was assumed to be because the correct outward forms had not been properly observed. It did not matter in the least to the Romans whether those performing sacrifices believed in what they were doing. This was completely irrelevant; all that mattered was that the outward actions should be correct.

Myths may change and decay; they seldom vanish without trace. In Britain today, we are still able to detect the later avatars of the mythic archetypes which have had such a profound effect upon our national psyche. Should you suspect that the horned god Cernunnos has now been lost without trace, then try this simple experiment: hand a pencil and paper to a 10-year-old child and ask him to draw the devil. He will produce a crude image of a human figure with horns sprouting from his head. The supernatural, horned demi-god is still a powerful part of this country's cultural baggage.

One more example should be sufficient to make the point. Since the coming of the Cro-Magnons across the grassy plain which would one day become the North Sea, we have in this country had a fear of newcomers from the East. They disrupt our lives with their disturbing ideas and newfangled ways of doing things. Sometimes they are bringing agriculture, on other occasions Christianity or literacy. Our newspapers today are still full of these newcomers. The idea that incoming strangers from the East have arrived with a new religion is not in the least a modern one. Whether it is Christianity or Islam and regardless of whether it has been brought by Romans or Saxons, Arabs or Jews, the outsider with new ideas has been a stock figure in our collective unconscious for over 30,000 years.

8

Wells, Mazes and Maypoles

We have mentioned in passing various features of London such as wells and mazes, some of which are often found near to later Christian places of worship. It is time to look at these in a little detail and see how they fit into the sacred world which lies beneath the streets of the city. We shall start with wells.

As with many pre-Christian religious sites, wells have a dual nature, the purely functional one of providing water for the community and also a religious or other worldly aspect. The religious element is derived from the fact that wells, which entail the digging of deep shafts in the earth, are an intrusion into the world below, that same world of gods and the dead to which rivers are the entrance. Forcing one's way into the underworld in this way, whether through well-digging or mining, can be a hazardous business. Apart from the obvious risks of cave-ins and other physical dangers, there is the very real chance of offending the deities or spirits whose realm is being invaded in this way. These entities must be propitiated by appropriate gifts and sacrifices at every stage of the procedure. Neolithic mines are often like underground shrines or chapels. It is plain that those digging there were careful to show their respect for the forces whose territory they were violating. Great care was taken to restore the land to the condition in which it had been found. This meant laboriously refilling galleries which had been worked out. Offerings were left in these closed off galleries as well, presumably to thank the gods for allowing men to take the flints or copper from their land.

In the flint mines of Grime's Graves in Norfolk, we see this ritual activity clearly. Every mine was returned to its natural state by being filled in with the chalk dug from the next mine. Just as in the well-closing ceremonies at which we shall look below, it seems to have been thought hazardous to leave an opening to the underworld. Such a shaft was like a gateway to the world below and there was no telling what might escape from these holes. In the mines themselves, there is abundant evidence that rituals were carried out as part and parcel of the actual process of extracting the seams of flint from the surrounding chalk. The walls are covered in strange graffiti, hearths are found, as though meals were prepared and eaten in the cramped and dark galleries and human remains, most notably skulls, are found.

It is unlikely that anybody would wish to light a fire and cook food in the low galleries of a Neolithic flint mine unless there was a pressing reason to do so. It would make far more sense to do any cooking in the open air. The most likely explanation is that these were ritual meals, designed to be shared with ancestors and the spirits who inhabited the underworld. A flint or chalk mine exists in London: Jack Cade's Cavern, which has already been mentioned. This network of galleries, which has never been examined by archaeologists, looks from photographs taken in 1938 to be very similar to prehistoric chalk mines found throughout Kent and in other parts of south-east England.

Intriguingly, those surveying it shortly before the outbreak of the Second World War found that the walls were covered with graffiti. Much of this was from the eighteenth and nineteenth century, at the time that it was open as a tourist attraction and nightclub, but some appeared to be older. Of great interest was a prominent carving of a horned human figure which covered most of one wall. Now one can readily imagine a visitor to these caves scratching their initials in the soft chalk or even taking the time to carve the year that they were there. It is hard to see even the most tolerant guide allowing a party of visitors to undertake a large scale bas relief of a horned god or devil though! If, as seems likely, this was a Neolithic mine then the representation of the horned god probably belongs to the same period. This may have been not merely a mine but a cult centre in its own right. That this is possible is suggested by another point which we shall come to shortly.

Water was drawn from wells; water which properly belonged to the spirits. Payment must be made for this vital resource, not every time a bucket was drawn from the well, but certainly at regular intervals. One of the most remarkable things which archaeologists have found when excavating old wells from this period is that all seem to be choked with votive offerings. These range from pins and coins to statues and human skulls. It seems to have been quite a common practice to cast a decapitated head into ancient British wells. Generally, only one skull is found for each well, suggesting that this may have been a one-off sacrifice or offering, perhaps made either when first the well had been dug and before it had been used or perhaps as part of the closing ceremonies when it was abandoned.

The custom of casting votive offerings into wells has not quite died out, especially in the so-called Celtic Fringe. In parts of Ireland and Scotland there are wells where rags are tied to nearby trees or offerings thrown in. Pins are considered the most appropriate votive offering and they are bent before being cast in. This precisely mirrors the treatment of the bronze swords and spearheads which are found in rivers and lakes. By bending the pin, one ends its practical use and declares it to be only for the spirit of the well or river.

In addition to wells, ritual shafts were also being dug with apparently the sole purpose of depositing goods as offerings for the spirits. Our view of the significance of much of what was being done in prehistoric Britain in general and London in particular has undergone a revolution in the last few decades. For many years, every time a buried hoard of metal was unearthed, the assumption was that it had been hidden and the owner intended to return for it at a later date. Glorious examples of bronze helmets and shields fished out of the Thames were thought to have been simply lost. When things were found buried in the silt at the foot of Roman wells, it was taken for granted that they had been dropped by careless people who were drawing water from the well. In short, researchers were using a modern perspective to shed light upon what they were discovering from thousands of years ago. When a hoard of ritual vessels were found in 2007 at the bottom of Roman well on the banks of the Walbrook, a newspaper referred to a 'Washing up scam', the implication being that somebody had chucked the things down the well to avoid having to go to the trouble of washing them. The writer of this headline was not, of course, advancing this as a serious theory to explain the finds, but he was really doing exactly what archaeologists have been doing for years, which is using twentieth- or twenty-first-century thought processes to get a handle on the behaviour of those who lived in the pre-Christian era. There are pitfalls in this approach.

Obtaining water, flint and metal from the earth was not seen as simply exploitation of the land. Rather, it was a process of trade. Goods were removed from the underworld and replaced with other things which the gods or the spirits of the dead might wish to have. Water was drawn from wells and coins were thrown in periodically as payment. If extra favour was required from the goddess, then a special gift might be sent to her world. This trading with the earth itself seems to have been common from the earliest times in London. The Thames was a source of flint, which was washed into the river by tributaries flowing through chalk and flint rich land. Flint nodules were picked up from the foreshore and worked into weapons and tools. Some of these artefacts would be returned to the river as offerings, probably in thanks for the provision of the raw material in the first place. This idea, that the earth must not simply be exploited ruthlessly without a thought for what is being taken, resonates in the modern mind. Organisations such as Greenpeace and Friends of the Earth express broadly similar sentiments. After all, it is thought to be a good, praiseworthy and responsible thing for mining and logging companies to restore the land to its original appearance once they have completed their industrial activities. This might be why neo-paganism is enjoying something of a resurgence in some quarters. The respect for the earth, sea and rivers, which was once such an integral part of everyday belief, seems to many today to be no more than common sense.

The rituals which we see in connection with wells have very old origins. When archaeological examination was being conducted of the area which would become

Terminal 5 at Heathrow airport, a number of water holes were found. These are too shallow to be called wells and are really no more than deep holes dug near rivers or marshes. They are sometimes lined or surrounded with wickerwork or wooden planks and are used just like wells. Those found beneath Terminal 5 were dated to about 3800 BC. They contained broken pottery and wooden objects, quite plainly ritual depositions of the sort seen 4000 years later in Roman wells in London: continuity of custom over an incredibly long period of time.

Old wells in London were frequently associated with a particular goddess or saint. Perhaps because these are essentially holes, wells are always associated with female deities. Some standing stones are similarly seen as being masculine. In the West Country, one such stone is known locally as 'Nick's Prick', the Nick being Old Nick or the devil. We will examine one particular well in detail, although its story is typical of many London wells. On the bank of the River Fleet, not far from the point where it entered the Thames, was a well dedicated to Bride. Bride is a variant form of the name Briget or Bridget. It may also be cognate with Brigantia, the goddess who we have seen earlier as being connected with the River Brent in West London. The Bride well near Fleet Street was a holy well which gave its name to a palace and prison which were later built nearby. In the late eighteenth century, the term 'Bridewell' became a synonym for prisons in London.

Near to the location of Bride's well, a church was built, St Bride's in Fleet Street. This is a classic case of the process described in Chapter 5, where a goddess metamorphoses into a human. Bride changed in the sixth century from a deity into a Christian saint, St Bridget. Wells and shrines which had previously been sacred to the goddess Bride/Brigantia/Briget were rededicated during this time to Bridget, who was supposedly a Druid's daughter who converted to Christianity. This leads us by a somewhat circuitous route to the discovery of another little part of the ritual landscape of prehistoric London.

During the Blitz in the Second World War, St Bride's church was almost destroyed by the bombing. All that remained was a burnt out shell. During the extensive rebuilding, traces were found of previous churches on the site of Wren's church. The earliest of these was dated to the seventh or eighth century AD. To the surprise of everybody, the remains of a far earlier structure were uncovered: a Roman building from the second century. The floor of this building may be seen in *colour plate 19*. The reason that the discovery of a Roman building here was unexpected can be understood readily if we look at the map in *figure 11*. The Roman city wall ended halfway up Ludgate Hill, where there was a gate. The road from this gate, Akeman Street, led to the west of England. It crossed the Fleet River by a bridge and followed the line of Fleet Street west. The building uncovered in the crypt of St Bride's was thus not only outside the city wall but on the wrong side of the Fleet. *Colour plate 13* shows how this area may have looked during the Roman occupation. The city of Londinium can be seen on the right and the Fleet enters the Thames outside the city wall. To the left, on the opposite bank of the Fleet from Londinium, is a small building. This stood on the site of St Bride's church. It is unlikely that anybody would be building a house outside the walls of Londinium, which leads us to ask what sort of building this might have been. The obvious solution would be that this was a Romano-Celtic temple or shrine connected with the worship of Bride or Brigantia. The fact that a well dedicated to this goddess was to be found nearby makes this by far the likeliest explanation. Just as any travellers approaching Londinium by road from Dover would find that the first building they encountered was a temple next to Watling Street as it passed through Greenwich, so too would anybody approaching the city from the west be sure to pass the temple to Bride or Brigantia just outside the city wall.

We have seen how newer religions have a habit of supplanting older ones by taking over their shrines and holy places. Christianity has always been very good at this, but the appropriation takes other forms than just hijacking this well or that hill. Goddesses are adopted and reduced in status to mere mortals and festivals are also purloined and renamed. Imbolc is the Celtic spring festival and falls on 2 February. It is known as *Oimelc*, ewe's milk, as well as Imbolc, because this is the time of year that the ewes begin lactating in preparation for the lambing season ahead. This day was sacred to Brigantia, which fitted neatly when St Brigit arrived: 2 February just became St Brigit's day. As a spring celebration, candles were paraded at Imbolc and the Christians kept this aspect of the festival, calling it Candlemas instead and incorporating it neatly into the church calendar. A later avatar of Imbolc is to be found in Groundhog Day in the United States, when hibernating animals emerge and their shadow may or may not be seen, thus allowing the remaining days of winter to be predicated. It is not by chance that 2 February is Groundhog Day. In Europe, this old wives' tale was connected with badgers and bears, and Candlemas was the time when one watched the weather in this way to see how soon spring would be coming.

Returning to St Bride's, this furnishes us with several classic examples of continuity of use in spatial and temporal terms. Firstly there, there is, of course, the physical appropriation of a site; in this case an ancient well. The church building now covers the well itself. Secondly, there is the hijacking of a goddess and demoting her to mortality, while at the same time claiming her for the Christian faith. Then again, the time of year for celebrating this goddess has also been taken over. Imbolc or Oimelc was a festival which, like Samhain, took place in a liminal zone of the changing year. It fell between winter and spring and was the hinge upon which the agricultural calendar turned. The sheep produced milk in expectation of the birth of lambs, the first flowers appeared, life was returning to the land.

At St Bride's, a door was actually knocked through the church wall so that processions could take place to the well in honour of Bride/Briget/Brigantia. This was a few years before the Tudor period. St Bride's well was still being used as a source of water in the area until well into the nineteenth century.

There is an even more remarkable and surprising continuity to be found in connection with this pagan shrine. Bride or Bridget was a goddess of fertility. Her sacred wells were thought by some to be a cure for barrenness in women. The well beneath St Bride's church was therefore almost certainly connected with fertility and procreation. In the eighteenth century, a baker's apprentice called Thomas Rich, who lived near Fleet Street, hit upon the idea of creating a wedding cake based upon the spectacular steeple of St Bride's. This steeple may be seen in *colour plate 14*. Thomas Rich died in 1811, but today his design for wedding cakes is still in fashion throughout the western world. So an architectural detail from the latest avatar of a shrine to the fertility goddess Bride is to this day a prominent feature of celebrations for many of those being married.

The custom of throwing coins into wells while begging favours of the gods is still extant in this country and other parts of Europe. Not only coins and skulls have been recovered from old wells in London. Southwark Cathedral is a very old church which is next to Duke street Hill in an area of early Roman settlement on the south bank of the Thames. As with so many important churches in London, it was almost certainly built on the site of an existing pre-Christian shrine. Traces of a Roman building have been found beneath the cathedral, together with an extremely ancient disused well.

Colour plate 10 shows a section of Roman flooring from beneath Southwark Cathedral. At the bottom of the well was a statue of a British hunter god, accompanied by two dogs. It may well be Cunomaglos, the Lord of the Hunt. This god, who is known only from a single inscription found in Wiltshire, was seemingly identified by the Romans with their own god Apollo (*colour plate 15*). Why anybody would drop this statue into a well is something of a mystery. One possible explanation is that it was hidden in the well during the ascendancy of Christianity in this country. The sculptures from the temple of Mithras on the bank of the River Walbrook were buried for this reason. More likely though is that it was thrown into the well as part of the rites conducted at the closing down of the well.

I mentioned in the introduction how the custom of throwing coins down near the site of the old well at Southwark has recently revived. A shaft which was dug for archaeological research during the building of an extension to the cathedral now serves the purpose of a well shaft.

Wells that were in use at that time that Londinium was flourishing also show signs of ritual use. In addition to coins and the odd human skull, such things as a statue of Minerva have been found at the bottom of a well from the City of London. The head of this statuette had been broken off and this was thought by archaeologists to have been a deliberate act, a ritual of destruction before closing up the well. Since, as we have seen, wells were regarded as an intrusion into the underworld, it was only logical that steps should be taken to close them down before abandoning them. Unless the correct rituals were observed, then the old well would act as a conduit between the world of the dead and our world. There was no telling what forces could escape from such a place. The nearest parallel in our technological age would be leaving a bare, live wire exposed. It would be an accident waiting to happen.

Some of the sacrifices made during the closing down ceremonies for a well could be substantial. A dig at Drapers Gardens, on the bank of the Walbrook, came across a disused well with an archaeological treasure trove lying at the bottom. A set of metal cauldrons, buckets, bowls and utensils, all in perfect condition, were found. They were made of a copper alloy and due to the waterlogged condition of the site they were not corroded. The first theory was that these items might have been hidden in the well by Romans fleeing the city during the collapse of Londinium in the fourth or fifth century AD, but this seems unlikely. They would have been all but impossible to retrieve at a later date and there was another factor which militated against this explanation. These vessels seem to have been religious objects. Some were the sort of thing that was used to pour libations to the gods, while others were shallow bowls associated with ritual cleansing. Almost certainly, these were thrown into the well as a gift to the underworld.

It is more than a little curious that the cult figure recovered from the well beneath Southwark Cathedral should have featured dogs. In addition to human skulls, a number of London wells have been found to contain dog skulls and some have contained a number of skeletons of whole dogs. This can hardly be chance. Cunomaglos was Lord of the Hunt and invariably accompanied by his dogs. Did his presence in the Southwark well and the discovery of dogs' skulls in others suggest some sort of connection with hunting and wells? The old British saying about a dog being a man's best friend dates perhaps from the very distant past. The connection of dogs with hunting and the British obsession with the animal may be bound up together.

Greenwich boasted a very strange well, one which has not been seen for many years. It is hidden within Jack Cade's caverns near Greenwich Park. The smallest of the caverns is reached by a long narrow passageway and was known as the Well Chamber. That a well should be dug in a cave is unusual and nothing is known of the story behind this shaft. When the caves were surveyed in 1938, it was simply recorded. It is, of course, perfectly possible that this well was dug during the Victorian heyday of the caverns, when they were being used as a nightclub. Equally possible is that this is ritual shaft of some sort dating from the time that the caverns were in use as mines. *Figure 17* shows the chalk escarpment beneath which these caverns may be found.

One or two of these old holy wells are still visible today. In Farringdon Lane, in Clerkenwell, is such a well. It can be seen by looking through the window of a modern office block. Like many so-called holy wells, this one was commandeered by a Christian religious house.

We shall look at one more holy well, one which brings us to Thorney Island and links neatly with another of the recurring themes of London's ritual

17 The chalk escarpment of the Point. Beneath this geological feature are to be found caverns and a well

landscape: the maze. There was once a sacred spring or holy well in Dean's Yard at Westminster Abbey. We know nothing at all about the history of this well, other than the fact that it was located on Thorney Island. A short distance away, a maze is shown in a map of the area made in the mid-seventeenth century. This was located next to Tothill Field, alongside the Tothill itself. Tothill Fields are still fields – playing fields belonging to Westminster School (see *18*).

In Chapter 1, we saw that three of the natural hills in central London had mazes on or near them. Now we see a maze established next to an artificial hill. Is this a coincidence? If not, what can the significance of these mazes be? The motif of the maze recurs again and again, not only in Britain, but also throughout the whole of Europe. In the next chapter we shall see a fanciful reason for the prevalence of the maze in this country. This is founded upon the idea that the Trojans built the first city on the site of London and that the maze was bound up with their historical origins. Few people take such notions seriously today. A more

18 Tothill Fields today

serious idea which has been put forward is that mazes are symbolic representations of the sacred groves of the Druids. In this view, the shrubby maze is seen as
being a little grove of the sort where Celtic religious ceremonies and sacrifices
were conducted. This is, at least superficially, convincing.

We know that most of the religious and ritual activity in prehistoric Britain
took place in the open air. This is in sharp contrast to the situation today, where
practically all religious observance takes place in special buildings. This is such a
great difference that we must stop for moment and consider how and why our
mode of worship has changed.

The first buildings in this country were primitive shelters designed to protect
one or two people from the wind and rain. The earliest such structures were
probably so small that it would be impossible to stand upright within them.
Think of a one-person tent. Later, they became a little more spacious, but still
with room only for a family. It made sense if a large group of people were going
to gather together for any purpose to do so out of doors. Clearings in forests were
perhaps the first places where groups assembled in one place to worship; later,
special locations such as causewayed enclosures and henges were constructed. The
forest clearing, though, remained in use until the time of the Druids, who, we are
assured by classical writers, were fond of trees and groves. We see the same principle at work with the sacred groves of ancient Greece.

Much of Britain was covered with forest during the Neolithic and Bronze
Age and a lot of this was oak. Epping Forest on the edge of London gives us
a good idea what a lot of the country would have looked like in those days:
many oak trees and a fair scattering of hornbeam and beech as well. The Celtic
Druids preferred oak groves for their rituals, which, according to some Roman
writers, included human sacrifice. Groves were without doubt popular places for

religious activities both in the classical world and also in that part of the eastern Mediterranean, which we call the Middle East. The Bible mentions sacred
groves and makes it clear that they are not to be encouraged. Either because
the Canaanites and Philistines used such places or because they were a favourite of the Greeks, whose pernicious influence the Jewish leaders were keen to
minimise, cutting down sacred groves was something which the prophets of Israel
regularly advocated.

Perhaps shrubby mazes could have been planted as miniature groves, symbol-
ising clearings in the forest? If so, then they might simply crop up throughout
London's history in the way that other motifs recur again and again at intervals,
just like the throwing of offerings into rivers and wells. If this were the case, then
it would not be the least bit surprising to find them near sacred places or on the
slopes of hills. Let's look at a few of these mazes and see if we can fathom out their
significance.

The district of Pentonville stands on a hilltop rising to about 130ft. It is situated about a mile and a half from the Thames. On Pentonville road itself, a stone's
throw from the Angel tube station, is a covered grass underground reservoir.
Those passing it each day probably hardly notice it, but this grassy mound marks
the very summit of the hill. The reservoir was placed there because a cave already
existed on this spot, known as Merlin's Cave. A short distance away in Rosebury
Street is the Sadler's Wells theatre, named after another holy well that was rediscovered in the eighteenth century and supposedly had medicinal properties. St
John's priory was built over this well; yet one more example of the church com-
mandeering a pre-existing holy place. Across the Pentonville Road from Merlin's
Cave, a maze once stood in White Conduit Street.

This combination of hilltop, holy well and Christian foundation is a familiar
one to us. It sometimes indicates a prehistoric, pagan place of worship. The presence of a cave associated with the greatest of ancient British magicians is curious
and could suggest a very old site.

Near Duke Street Hill, in Southwark, was another maze, this one in the garden
of Princess Mary, later to become infamous as Bloody Queen Mary. The whole
area here has for thousands of years been important from a religious point of
view: Southwark Cathedral, a Roman well, Romano-Celtic temples, barrows and
prehistoric burials, all clustered around a hilltop.

A third maze is shown in a seventeenth-century view of Tothill Fields on
Thorney Island. The open ground near this maze was used for the 'Game of Troy'.
This was a ritual dance in which some riders on horseback and others on foot
weaved in and out in ever decreasing circles as though spiralling in to the centre of
a labyrinth. In other words, it was a highly ritualised and symbolic representation of
people finding their way to the centre of a maze. Virgil describes the Game of Troy
and whether or not it actually originated in that city, it is certainly very ancient.
Dances or processions of this sort are known to have been practised at other mazes

in this country. A significant point about the Game of Troy is that in Rome it was performed as part of funeral ceremonies. This has led some to suppose that the movement of the dancers through elaborate circular pathways symbolised the passage of a soul from the world of the living to the land of the dead.

Finally, a turf maze was to be found in Greenwich, by the road now called Maze Hill. Turf mazes, all of which are spirals rather than the more familiar Greek key design, are found in different places, both in this country and the rest of Europe, principally Scandinavia.

Before going any further, perhaps it might be as well to say a few words about the different kinds of maze. Basically, all mazes belong to one of two types: the spiral or the key pattern. In the former, one continuous path leads unerringly to the centre. It is impossible to become lost; one simply follows a predetermined course. This is the most ancient design for mazes. Some of the earliest known examples of the spiral maze are carved on a rock near Tintagel Castle in Cornwall. These looped, spiralling patterns almost certainly date from the Neolithic era some 5000 years ago.

The other type is the sort which most of us think of when we talk of a maze. The key pattern, which is believed to be of Greek origin, is a more rectangular formation which meanders this way and that. So the journey to the centre of a meander maze, its alternative name, is beset with dead ends, false turns and branching paths. In sharp contrast to spiral mazes, in which one must inevitably reach the centre, it is theoretically possible to wander in a meander maze and never find the correct route. This is the form of all modern mazes, by which I mean those constructed in the last 500 years or so. Perhaps one of the best known examples is situated at the old palace of Hampton Court on the banks of the River Thames. Now Hampton Court and all similar hedge mazes wherein the visitor might become lost are similar not only in design, but also in purpose; they are built to amuse.

The earliest mazes, however, were not constructed simply to provide a merry diversion on a Sunday afternoon. Their purpose was altogether subtler and more mysterious than mere entertainment. This is typified in turf mazes, a few of which still exist, such as that near the village of Wing in Leicestershire. Of unknown but undoubtedly great age, this is a spiral design 30 yards in diameter, cut to a depth of 3in in the surrounding turf. Here, unlike the great hedge mazes such as Hampton Court, the whole design is visible at a glance. There is no mystery about which path to take because there is only one, looping and curving back on itself as it leads inexorably to the centre of the circle. We note that a prehistoric burial mound is right next to the maze at Wing, suggesting an association with death.

To the sophisticated, modern visitor there is something more than a little puzzling about a maze in which one cannot lose one's way. What could possibly be the point of walking a predetermined course along a shallow bank of turf? The answer is that these proto-mazes were places not of amusement but of ritual.

Exactly what form these rituals took, we can only guess; possibly they symbolised the passage of the soul from birth to death or from death to paradise.

Turf mazes of this sort were once a common sight not only in Britain but throughout the whole of Northern Europe. Indeed, in Wales shepherds used to cut mazes into the grass as a pastime while watching their flocks. They called these miniature labyrinths *Caerdroia*, which is Welsh for City of Troy.

Although we use the term 'labyrinth' for all kinds of mazes, it may properly only be applied to the spiral design with one path to the centre. This is also the most ancient design. According to legend, this design was devised by Daedelus, father of Icarus, in order to construct a safe prison for the Minotaur. It is a curious coincidence that our examination of this motif, found repeatedly in London, should once again bring us back to the image of a half human creature with horns.

This pattern, the swirling and curving lines moving inexorably in one direction, looping backwards and forwards as it draws to the centre, is found on many megaliths and tombs. One clue as to its original purpose may be found by looking to Scandinavia, where in coastal regions near fishing villages the building of such designs has been a custom for countless centuries. There too, they are known by names which translate as Troy towns, but the real meaning of the expression there concerns not Troy, but trolls. The aim of these little mazes is to trap trolls and other evil spirits and keep them bound up in the labyrinths so that they cannot roam free and cause mischief to those at sea. Could this be the reason that prehistoric people engraved these designs on tombs and near to sacred places? Perhaps they were intended to stop evil spirits from escaping from tombs?

In a number of old cathedrals, Chartres, at which we looked in Chapter 1, is a good example, spiral mazes are inlaid in the floor. Penitents would move along these mazes on their knees, making a symbolic pilgrimage. Some were known as Chemins de Jerusalem. This was just what some of the older turf mazes in this country were for. The purpose of the ritual might have been forgotten, but people would trudge along the path until the centre was reached. Since the spiral labyrinth design is far older than the Greek key pattern, it is possible that they are copies of the spiral motifs found in some prehistoric, chambered tombs. Were they intended to show the progress of the soul after death, as it struggled to reach paradise?

A full understanding of the meaning of the maze as it is seen in its earliest form requires us once again to abandon our twenty-first-century perspective and try to look at things from the point of view of those who first carved these designs on to the stones of their barrows or into the turf of hillsides. Engraving a complex spiral pattern into a slab of stone with only stone tools would be an immensely time-consuming undertaking. There must have been a powerful motive underlying such activity; a motive that was religious and connected with those whose physical remains were stored in the tomb.

For the Neolithic community, death itself was not the end of life. Rather, the moment of death was the prelude to an in-between time, before the spirit of the person who had died could finally leave the body and go wherever the spirits of the dead went according to the belief system of the time. We know that corpses were not placed into tombs or buried at once. Some process took place, probably excarnation, before the remains were seen as finally dead and ready to be disposed of. The period between death and burial was a special sort of liminal time, a time when the dead person's spirit worked through some process before being freed completely from its body.

The mortuary enclosures which we discussed above might have played a role in this in-between time. Once the person had stopped breathing, the transition from being completely alive to fully dead and in the realm of the spirits would begin. It was the beginning of a journey or pilgrimage, rather than, as we see it today, a sharp and immediate change in status from living to dead. It is likely that excarnation played a part in this progression. It was definitely the case that only when all the flesh had gone from the body was it ready to be placed in a barrow or otherwise disposed of. Perhaps until this had happened, the corpse was not truly accepted as being dead.

All this brings us back both to the maze which seems to have cropped up by the hills of central London and also to the cursus which once ran for miles beneath Heathrow airport. The most likely explanation for the spiral, single pathway maze or labyrinth is, without doubt, that it represents a journey or progression, rather than a puzzle. This is where a person or spirit will go, not a course that may or may not be followed. The patterns in passage tombs like Newgrange in Ireland probably reflect this. They show what will be happening to the spirit or soul of the dead occupant of the tomb, the path which he will be following to salvation or rest. As such, the spiral design can be seen as a cult sign. This is shorthand for the path taken by the spirits of the dead. It is also the design for a pathway in this world, a turf maze, that mourners can follow in sympathy with the dead person, reflecting their own journey to rest.

Although they are lost now, it is likely that at one time there were many spiral turf mazes in this country, including some in London itself. These were created not for amusement but for some quasi-religious purpose which is not wholly clear to us now. These mazes would probably have been located near to wells, barrows and hilltops as part of the wider ritual landscape. Now turf mazes need to be scoured regularly if they are to maintain their design. Times change and it is quite conceivable that when the meander maze came into fashion in this country, these might have been planted over old turf mazes as a replacement. By this time, the original, deeper meaning of the old mazes would have been lost or forgotten.

The cursuses too, which are dotted around the countryside as part of ritual landscapes, might have served a similar function to the spiral pathways of the old mazes. Some lead from one section of the landscape to another and it has been hypothesised that these are paths from the land of the living to the realm of the dead. When the Stanwell cursus was found, it was so straight and meticulously constructed that it was at first thought to be a Roman road. That it was a road in the way that we now think of roads, that is to say a strip of land which allows people to travel easily from one place to another, is very unlikely. It did not lead from anywhere to anywhere else in particular. The land around this part of West London is dry enough. It is not marshy and waterlogged like those parts of the city further east and so there would be no reason at all to go to all the trouble of raising a road up from the ground in this fashion.

It is likely that the cursus at Stanwell was intended to allow the spirits of the dead to move from one part of the landscape to another, for reasons at which we can only guess. An interesting feature is that at one point, the cursus has a number of postholes running alongside it. These seem to have been for a line of poles or posts like the avenue at the Shepperton henge. It is impossible now to know just what these tall poles were supposed to signify. They may have been phallic symbols, totem poles or simply structures designed to reach as high to the heavens as possible. Sacred poles of this sort are mentioned and forbidden in the Bible. Chapter 31 of the second book of Chronicles tells us that the people of Israel broke down the stone pillars of other religions and also tore down the altars on high places and cut down the 'sacred poles'.

Just as certain springs and lakes were regarded as holy in ancient times, so too were particular trees. It is quite possible that these 'sacred poles' were representations of special trees. It has been suggested that standing stones are also intended to symbolise trees. It is instructive to look again to Northern Europe in this context. As late as the eighth century, people in Germany were erecting tree trunks in this way and treating them as the centre of their religious practices. We remember the tree trunks which were placed upright on Salisbury Plain 10,000 years ago and it is hard not to conclude that this was the same custom. We are irresistibly reminded of the 6500-year-old posts at Vauxhall. Could they be part of the same tradition? The Germans called these tree trunks *Irminsuls* and it is suspected that they may represent the Ash Yggdrasil or World Tree, which in Norse mythology linked the underworld with our own living world.

In AD 772, Charlemagne destroyed a famous Irminsul belonging to the Saxons. This was apparently a shaped tree trunk set up in a forest clearing and worshipped by the local tribesmen. Whatever these 'sacred poles' might have been either in prehistoric Britain, Biblical Israel or dark-age Europe, London has a long history of erecting them. Several became permanent and well-known features of the city. We know them as maypoles.

The first written reference to a maypole in London is from the fifteenth century. A famous maypole stood on the highest part of the city at Cornhill. This in itself, the erecting of a strange structure of unknown purpose on the top of one of the highest parts of the City of London, should alert us to the possibility that there is a ritual element to what we are seeing. A church nearby was known at one time as St Andrew Cornhill. Because of the proximity and height of the maypole – it was taller than the church itself – the church became known by the name that it bears today; St Andrew Undershaft. Maypoles became the focus for much drunkenness and general disorder during the fifteenth and sixteenth centuries. Celebrations for May Day in London in 1517 ended in riot and mayhem, earning this May Day the title of the 'Evil May Day'. Some of the ringleaders of this event were subsequently executed.

These maypoles were not erected only for a week or so, but were permanent fixtures. That they had some sort of pre-Christian association is shown by the fate of the Cornhill maypole. In 1549, the local priest denounced it as a heathen idol and it was chopped up for firewood. The Puritans too disapproved of the licentiousness which became associated with the revels of May Day and this led to the destruction of all the maypoles of London. In 1583 Philip Stubbes, a prominent commentator on the Elizabethan London scene, called the maypole 'this stinking idol'. He drew attention to the number of young women who lost their virginity during the May Day celebrations.

Oliver Cromwell banned dancing around the maypole entirely and most existing ones were chopped down. After the restoration of the monarchy, though, new and larger maypoles were set up in London, including one on the Strand which was 134ft tall. It is very likely that these poles were the latest manifestations of a practice which dates back in this country at least 10,000 years.

9

On the Fringe: Some Outlandish Ideas about Prehistoric London

We have reconstructed the early history of London, using a variety of sources, including archaeological evidence and written accounts from classical writers. The picture which has emerged is an intriguing one, showing prehistoric men and women living cheek by jowl with their gods and ancestors. These early inhabitants of the Thames valley shaped their landscape in various ways and attributed supernatural influences to every aspect of their lives. It is a fascinating process, attempting to recreate the mythology and religious beliefs of our forebears by studying earthworks and old skulls. Not, however, nearly fascinating enough for some, who have over the centuries preferred to weave dreams and fantasies about the origins of London.

There may have been some excuse for spinning yarns about London's distant past in the dark ages when the first efforts were made to write a history of the city. After all, these medieval writers had little authentic material upon which to work. London at that time was surrounded by the ruins of great palaces, walls and temples. It was impossible to say by whom these had been built, whether Roman, Greek or even Trojan.

The idea that London was founded by the Trojans is a very old one, dating back to the time of the Saxons. The whole country was at that time in a state of flux, with control swaying between Saxon and Dane. Perhaps some writers thought that it would be nice if Britain could be provided with a noble history which would prove that their nation was the natural successor to Rome.

We have looked at a few of Geoffrey of Monmouth's ideas and found that buried within his stories are occasional authentic fragments of folk memories which have their roots in the Iron Age or earlier. It is time now to examine in detail one of his strangest and most controversial claims: that the City of London was founded not by the Romans but by descendents of a band of Trojan warriors who fled their city after its destruction by the besieging Greek forces. This is generally reckoned by historians to have occurred around 1200 BC. Geoffrey was not the first writer to have thought of claiming that his nation had been founded by noble Trojans.

Virgil, perhaps the greatest of Roman poets, wrote his masterpiece the *Aeneid* during the last 10 years of his life. Deliberately modelled on the *Iliad*, It tells the story of the escape of Aeneas, his family and friends from the sack of Troy. After many adventures, he found his way to Italy, where he married Lavinia, the only daughter of King Latinus. He was the ancestor of Romulus and Remus, legendary founders of the city of Rome. Virgil took some vague existing legends and wove them into a heroic epic in the style of Homer. The result is magnificent poetry and also a justification for the Roman subjugation of the known world.

Writing in the ninth century, a Welsh monk called Nennius took Virgil's story and expanded it. To be more precise, he added a sequel, which entailed Aeneas' grandson Brutus travelling to Britain and laying the foundation stone of the city of New Troy, which became in time London. Nennius, like Geoffrey of Monmouth 300 years later, denied inventing this story. According to him, these were simply old legends that he was setting down as he heard them. Here is the story as told by Nennius and expanded a few centuries later by Geoffrey.

Decades after Aeneas had settled in Italy, his grandson Sylvius became king. As in the Oedipus myth, Sylvius was inadvertently slain by his own son, Brut. Brut, or Brutus as he was also known, was horrified when he discovered what he had done and went for advice to the oracle and the temple of Diana. The oracle told him that he would have to leave Rome forever. However, his exile would lead to the birth of a new nation which would be even greater than Rome. In the words of the oracle:

Brut – past the realms of Gaul beyond the sunset,
Lieth an island girt about by ocean,
Guarded by ocean - erst the haunt of giants,
Desert of late and meet for this thy people,
Seek it! For there is thine abode for ever.
There, by thy sons shall Troy again be builded,
Herafter sovran in every land the wide world over.

Together with his faithful friend Corineus and a group of adventurous young men, Brutus set sail, landing eventually at Totnes in Devon in about 1000 BC. As he leapt ashore, Brutus landed on a granite boulder and it was while standing on this rock that he staked his claim to the country. The Brutus stone, as it is known, may still be seen in Fore Street in Totnes. From then on, the land which had been known as Albion was renamed Britain in memory of Brutus.

At this time Albion was populated by coarse and brutal giants, the debased remnants of the race of Bran. The greatest of these giants was known as

Gogmagog, and Corineus, a famous wrestler, fought with him and threw him to his death at Plymouth Hoe. When the time came to divide up the country, Corineus chose Cornwall for his share as it had the greatest number of giants and he wanted the sport of wrestling them all. When he had rid it of all the giants, Cornwall was named Corinia in his honour. This is reflected in the Celtic name for the county, Kernow.

Brutus meanwhile started his new kingdom on the site of present-day London, building a great city which he called Troy Novante, meaning New troy. Geoffrey says of Brutus' foundation of London, after he had been seeking the best site for his new capital:

> He visited every part of the land in search of a suitable spot. He came at length to the river Thames, walked up and down its banks and so chose a site suited to his propose. There he built his city and called it Troia Nova. It was known by this name for long ages after, but finally by a corruption of the word came to be called Trinovantum.

When the Romans arrived, they found a tribe of Britons living in the area called the Trinovantes. An old tradition says that they spoke a language very similar to Latin and that they shared many myths and legends with the invading Romans. Trinovante is believed by some to be a corruption of Troy Novante.

Brutus built his palace where the Guildhall now stands and also erected a temple to Diana on the crest of Ludgate Hill. When he died, his son Locrine became king. Locrine married Corineus' daughter Gwendoline, but he also had a mistress, Estrildis. Fearful of Gwendoline and her powerful father, Locrine kept Estrildis hidden in a vast labyrinth which he caused to be dug beneath Troy Novante. For seven years she lived there, guarded by Locrine's servants. She even bore him a child, Habren, or Sabrina in Latin.

When Corineus died, Locrine put aside Gwendoline and installed Estrildis as queen. The furious Gwendoline raised an army and attacked Troy Novante, killing Locrine. Estrildis and her child were now at Gwendoline's mercy. She had them both drowned in the River Severn, which was later named after Sabrina. Nereus the sea god took pity on Sabrina and turned her into a river goddess.

This then is the legend which Nennius and Geoffrey of Monmouth promoted in the Middle Ages. They also set out an entire subsequent dynasty of kings descended from Brutus. Lud, for example, supposedly reinforced the walls of Troy Novante and built a new gate, Ludgate. During his reign Troy Novante became known as Lud Din, Lud's City, which later became corrupted to London.

It has to be said that there is not a shred of evidence for these stories. The idea that London was a classical city with stone walls and temples before Caesar landed here is improbable in the extreme. Archaeologists have, at any rate, found no trace of this earlier city. It may have been possible when writing in Anglo-Saxon times to imagine that the remains of the ruined stone walls which encircled London had been built by the Trojans in 1000 BC, but the evidence now tells us that the Romans put them up some time in the second century AD. No trace of any buildings before the time of the Romans has ever been found, with the exception of a few postholes from wattle and daub huts.

How did Nennius and Geoffrey of Monmouth come up with this idea of New Troy? It is probably due to a combination of poor scholarship and a vivid imagination. Caesar described the Trinovantes, a tribe living in East Anglia, as a 'civitas', which a later translator decided to render as 'city'. Really, the word *civitas* means 'nation'. This simple error gave Geoffrey of Monmouth the opportunity to devise an entirely new and noble history for the British people.

Geoffrey of Monmouth's book, *Historia Regum Britanniae* or the *History of the Kings of Britain*, was the medieval equivalent of a bestseller, despite the fact that printing had not yet been invented in Europe when he wrote it. It was translated into Norman French, Welsh and Middle English, with several versions being produced in verse. For about 500 years after it was written, in roughly 1135, this was seen as the definitive history of Britain and the best account of London's origins which one could hope to read. By the middle of the seventeenth century, though, doubts about the authenticity of Geoffrey were widespread.

Even during Geoffrey of Monmouth's lifetime, there were those who doubted his claims. William of Newburgh, who lived at about the same time as Geoffrey, was scathing about the *Historia Regum Britanniae*, saying: 'Everything this man wrote about Arthur and his successors, or indeed about his predecessors from Vortigern onwards, was made up, partly by himself and partly by others, either from an inordinate love of lying, or for the sake of pleasing the Britons.'

Strong words indeed! Yet it is possible to have some sympathy for Geoffrey of Monmouth. He was living in a time when London was surrounded by the remnants of a mighty, stone-walled city, plainly constructed in the classical style. This was before the days of archaeology and he simply filled in gaps in the history with half remembered folklore and some embellishments of his own. Despite the harsh criticism which has been levelled against him, very little of his tales seem to have been invented from nothing. He was something of a jackdaw, taking a story here and an old legend there and embroidering the whole with his own not inconsiderable imagination.

In recent years, there has been an attempt to link the Trojan story to a very ancient London landmark: the London Stone, which is still to be found on the banks of the Walbrook in Cannon Street. The London Stone is an unremarkable, roughly rectangular block of limestone about the size of a microwave oven. It was mentioned by Shakespeare and has been in Cannon Street for at least a thousand years. Nobody knows where it came from or what its original purpose might have been. Since the Middle Ages, it has been a place where deals may be struck and oaths sworn. John Stow, an Elizabethan historian wrote:

standing in Walbrook, on the south side of this High Street, near unto the
Channel, is pitched upright a great stone called London Stone, fixed in the
ground very deep, fastened with bars of iron, and otherwise so strongly set that
if carts do run against it through negligence the wheels be broken, and the
stone itself unshaken. The cause why this stone was there set, the very time
when, or other memory thereof, is there none.

The most likely explanation for the London Stone is that it is a tiny fragment,
perhaps a gatepost, of the governor's palace which stood here in Roman times.
Another theory is that it was the milestone at the heart of Londinium, from
which all distances were measured by the Romans. There are legends connect-
ing the London Stone with Brutus the Trojan, but these only appear to go back
as far as the Celtic revival of the nineteenth century. The 'legend' is that because
Brutus received such encouraging advice from the oracle at the temple of Diana,
he swore an oath that when he had come into his inheritance, the new country
which he found beyond the Pillars of Hercules, he would build a magnificent
new temple in Diana's honour. This he did on the top of Ludgate Hill and the
London Stone is the remaining part of the altar from that temple.

   According to some modern writers, there is an old saying that:

   So long as the Stone of Brutus is safe,
   So long will London flourish.

This is stated to be a translation of a Celtic saying

   Tra maen Prydain
   Tra Illed Llydain.

In fact this is not an old legend at all. It dates no further back than 1862, when a
Welsh vicar who was living in London at the time, Rev. Richard Morgan, wrote
to a magazine with this story. Morgan was a great enthusiast for Celtic history and
author of a book called *The British Kymry,* in which he traced the history of the
British people from the Great Flood onwards. Another supposed legend, that the
London Stone was the stone from which Arthur pulled excalibur, is even more
recent. It is first found in a book published in 2002!

   Today, there are still those who subscribe to Geoffrey of Monmouth's fanciful history. On websites and in books and magazines, the idea that London was
founded by Trojan exiles is discussed as though it were solid, historical fact. The
truth is, there is not a single piece of evidence to back up this notion. Occasionally,
anomalous objects are found in London. For example, a two-handed drinking
vessel has been dredged from the Thames which might well have come from Asia
Minor. Glass beads of a pattern found in the remains of Troy have also turned up.

These do not, however, lead orthodox archaeologists to hypothesise about a possible Middle Eastern wave of settlers in the area around 1200 BC. Far more likely is that these items were acquired by trade.

As well as those who subscribe to the theory of a Trojan origin for London are the new wave of 'Celtomaniacs' who try to impose a Druidical narrative upon the city. These are people like the Druid Order, who were founded a century ago. They dress up in long white robes and parade on Primrose Hill to mark the autumn equinox. At the spring equinox, they hold ceremonies on Tower Hill.

A whole bogus history of London has been contrived by some Celtic enthusiasts, with folk etymology of London place names playing a big part. Take Pentonville, for instance. There was a holy well near the summit of this hill and a cave. A maze was planted nearby and it is quite likely that, in prehistoric times, this hill had some sort of significance as part of the wider ritual landscape of London. So far, we may confidently go; but not very much further. Pentonville itself is named after Henry Penton, an eighteenth-century developer who was responsible for the building over of this district. This prosaic and historically indisputable account has been jettisoned by those keen on Celtic culture in favour of an altogether more satisfying explanation. They claim that *Pen Ton* in Celtic meant 'hill head' and that this is the true origin of Pentonville.

Tower Hill has been identified as Bryn Gwynn, the White Mount and Parliament Hill is suggested as being a holy hill which gave its name to the entire city: Llan-Din. Tower Hill probably was important in prehistoric times, as were the other hills of the London area, Pentonville and Parliament Hill included. It is not inconceivable that it was the hill specified in the *Mabinogion* as the final resting place of Bran's head. From this, it is a long way to assigning every hill in London with a Celtic name and trying to connect them with particular festivals.

Nor is this the limit to the fantasies which have in the last few decades been woven about the capital. The story of the labyrinth beneath the streets of the city is also told on websites as though it were recognised and incontrovertible fact. Beneath London, according to these ideas is a vast network of tunnels and galleries, something like the catacombs of Rome. It should hardly be necessary to debunk such ideas. Rome is built upon solid rock, into which it has proved possible, but laborious, to carve tunnels. This is not and could never be the case with London. With the exception of outcrops of chalk here and there, the whole city is built upon soggy clay. A self-supporting tunnel through material of this type is a physical impossibility.

Alfred Watkins was a self-taught archaeologist. He was born in Hereford in 1855 and pursued a number of passions over the course of his long life. His family were prosperous, with businesses scattered across a wide area and so he had the time and money to follow a number of hobbies. One of these was photography and he was the inventor of a very small and accurate exposure meter. So successful was this that one was taken to the South Pole on Scott's expedition in 1912.

When he was approaching 70, Alfred Watkins was in Herefordshire when he had the sudden inspiration that the whole British landscape was crisscrossed with straight lines, dating from Neolithic times and composed of various ancient landmarks. These were old tracks and the various prehistoric monuments had acted as sighting points so that travellers could move from one part of the country to another without the need for compasses or signposts. This is not a particularly strange idea and there are certainly cases where tracks were arranged in this way. He wrote a book called *Early British Trackways*, which was published the following year in 1922 and then followed this up with his classic work, *The Old Straight Track*, in 1925. He devoted the rest of his life until his death in 1935 to expanding upon this idea. He coined the expression 'ley lines' to describe this phenomenon which he thought he had observed and ever since then his ley lines have been a favourite of those with a taste for esoteric matters.

It must be said at once that no mainstream archaeologists subscribes to Watkins' ideas. Part of the problem was that he cast his net very wide indeed in order to come up with landmarks which could in any sense be said to be in a straight line. He listed 17 markers which could be considered significant; these were, in descending order of importance: mounds, stones, circular moats, castles, beacons, traditional wells, pre-Reformation churches, crossroads, road alignments, fords, tree groups, single trees, dips in the skyline, track junctions, hill forts, ponds and square moats.

Many of these were what Watkins describes as 'evolved sites', places like St Paul's Cathedral which, although only dating from the Restoration itself, marks an ancient site. There are two things to bear in mind when looking at ley lines. First, the idea of Neolithic tracks across the countryside which use standing stones or other markers so that travellers can sight along them to keep in the right direction is not at all far fetched. Such markers exist and there are well-defined tracks or green lanes leading to important ancient locations like Grime's Graves. Secondly, the whole topic of ley lines has been taken over by those who believe in mysterious earth energies and Feng Shui. This means that it has passed from the realm of archaeology into pseudoscience and mysticism, which is a pity, because it has led many to dismiss Watkins' work out of hand.

How does all this relate to London? Alfred Watkins claimed to have identified a number of important ley lines in or leading to London. Other modern researchers have thought that they have uncovered patterns of lines which cover the capital in pentagrams and intricate networks of interlocking energy fields. A typical example of a Watkins ley line in London is the Strand Ley. This started at St Martin-in-the-Fields at Trafalgar Square. Although this is an eighteenth-century church, a place of worship has stood on the site for a thousand years or so. This is what Watkins meant by an 'evolved site'. During building work in the eighteenth century, an underground stream was found flowing beneath the foundations of St Martin. This was perhaps a tributary of the Tyburn. A Roman archway was also seen. All this might possibly indicate that the present church stood on a prehistoric cult site. Three other churches are in a straight line with St Martin-in-the-Fields. They are St Mary-le-Strand, St Clement Danes and St Dunstan's in Fleet Street. From here, a line can be extended all the way to Shoreditch in the East End, where it terminates at Arnold Circus – the site of a prehistoric mound, near which once stood a priory.

Now all this is interesting, but not particularly convincing. Readers might care to take a map of London and a ruler and then experiment by drawing straight lines. It is not hard to link important places in this way. For instance, one such line that some have thought significant is to be found by drawing a straight line between Tower Hill and Westminster Abbey. Amazingly, it passes through Southwark Cathedral! Since these are all definitely evolved sites, could this be another ley line? Few objective and hard-headed thinkers would be likely to concede that this may be so. After all, a straight line drawn anywhere at all in London is bound to link at least two or three churches, prehistoric sites, places where a subterranean stream flows, old wells, former sites of religious houses and many other places.

There is nothing improbable in the idea of a prehistoric track from one important place to another. A source of flint, such as Grime's Graves in Norfolk, most likely would have had tracks leading from it to various places. One such has, in fact, been hypothesised. 'Green lanes' are old tracks which are to be found in many parts of the countryside. They are the remains of pre-industrial roads which once linked farms and villages to larger centres of population. The green lanes which are to be found today are fragmentary and incomplete. They pass through farmland and across modern roads and really exist only in short stretches. In the hills above the market town of Waltham Abbey in Essex, which is on the outskirts of London, are several short stretches of green lanes. A line drawn between Grime's Graves flint mines and Westminster passes right through these green lanes, which are aligned along this route. Even more intriguingly, a pillar of puddingstone, a type of rock, is found on a hilltop by one section of this track. It could have been a sighting point for anybody making the journey from the flint mines to Thorney Island.

The sorts of tracks described above are one thing. The ley line hypothesis as it is talked of today is another thing entirely. If, as has been suggested here, London was a major cult centre in prehistoric times and a place of pilgrimage, then it is plausible that tracks converged from other parts of Britain. We know of at least one real road, that leading from Colchester to London, and there were perhaps others. In addition to the type of road needed for horses and carts, there would have been other, smaller tracks.

The problem with the London ley lines is that they have mutated from simple Neolithic tracks into channels for earth energy; the sort of things needing a dowser to be traced rather than an archaeologist.

Others have come up with notions about prehistoric London which might have some merit, but which need a good deal more research to establish. As we know, several places in West London, such as Caesar's Camp and the Shepperton henge were aligned to sunrise at special dates in the calendar. The claim has been made that a whole series of such places are to be found in the London area. Parliament Hill was, according to some Celtic enthusiasts, once called Llan Din and actually gave its name to London. Apparently if one stands on the top of this hill at dawn on the day of the winter solstice, then the sun appears to rise precisely above the hill at Pentonville. This coincidence led to the drawing of a line from Parliament Hill to Pentonville and then extending it towards the Thames. Lo and behold, it strikes Tower Hill and the site of the Tower of London. Since this is the supposed place where the head of Bran was buried, it has been suggested that Tower Hill itself may be partly artificial and that the area of the Tower of London was a cult centre.

Other supposed astronomical alignments include the fact that if one stands on Primrose Hill, a line drawn to Thorney Island and Westminster points to the summer solstice azimuth. The reader is not to suppose that I am asserting this to be true; merely that it has been claimed elsewhere. It has also been remarked that Arnold Circus, site of the old Friars' Mount, lies exactly due north of the Tower of London. Several books have been published in recent years which are predicated upon the existence of astronomical alignments of London's landmarks as well as their positioning according to principles akin to Feng Shui.

Another rich field for speculation and the spinning of theories about London's origins and early history lies in the eighteenth century Druidic revival which was called by some 'Celtomania'. Druidism became something of a craze during Victoria's reign and a society similar to the Freemasons flourished. This enjoyed considerable popularity, with even Winston Churchill becoming a member in 1908. The Ancient Order of Druids was actually founded in London in 1781 at the height of the enthusiasm for all things Celtic.

Ten years before *The Old Straight Track* was published, a woman called Elizabeth Oke Gordon, a devotee of Druidism, published *Prehistoric London: its Mounds and Circles*. This purported to be a history of ancient London. Gordon believed that Geoffrey of Monmouth was right about the Trojan origin of the British. She also subscribed to some of the ideas of the British Israelite movement, who believed that the lost tribes of Israel had found their way here and that the British were the heirs of King David.

Gordon detailed a number of stone circles which she claimed had once stood in London. One of these, similar to Stonehenge, she thought had existed where St Paul's Cathedral now stands. She suggested that the London Stone had at one time been the 'index stone' for this circle, a bit like the Heel Stone at Stonehenge. Gordon's book has been reprinted in recent years and her ideas enthusiastically embraced by those who find the real history of the capital a little lacklustre and wanting in romance.

The difficulty with accepting that stone circles once existed in London is that there is not a single piece of evidence for the notion. There is no source of stone near London and it was not until the Roman city of Londinium that we have any evidence of stonework in the city. A stone circle would surely have left at least some trace, even after a few thousand years.

This does not by any means exhaust the store of weird theories about prehistoric London, but since none of them are really tenable, or indeed supported by any evidence, there is little point in detailing every such fantasy. The history of London is fascinating enough, without dreaming up Trojan kings and Druid temples!

10

Walking the Ritual Landscape

A surprising amount of London's ancient ritual landscape remains to be seen today. The traces are, however, widely scattered and so it might be convenient to divide our exploration into five self-contained walks, which range from Greenwich in the east to Westminster in the West. What is very curious is that many of the prehistoric remains are completely unnoticed by anybody other than archaeologists. Greenwich Park, for example, is always bustling with tourists and yet all seem intent only upon visiting the Royal Observatory and nearby planetarium. A stone's throw from the planetarium, though, is a large chunk of the ritual landscape which once covered this whole area: a group of Bronze Age round barrows which have been reused by the Saxons. A few hundred yards away are the vestiges of a Romano-Celtic temple complex which were once the first buildings which any traveller from Dover would encounter when travelling to London. Similarly, in central London fragments of prehistoric history are lying openly for all to see. Most people simply walk past, unaware that the clues to their city's past are right in front of them.

Greenwich

We begin this walk from Greenwich High Road, which is a short distance from the Docklands railway station of Cutty Sark. We walk first up Croom's Hill, along the side of Greenwich Park. This is a very old road indeed. *Croom* in old Celtic meant 'crooked' and the road does bend and twist as it ascends. The suggestion has been made that the Celtic name makes this the oldest road in Britain still in use. At the top of the hill, we veer right into Cade Road and then carry on along Shooters Hill, until we reach a small road on the left called Point Hill. On the left is Blackheath, a grassy common. Walking down Point Hill will reveal to our left a

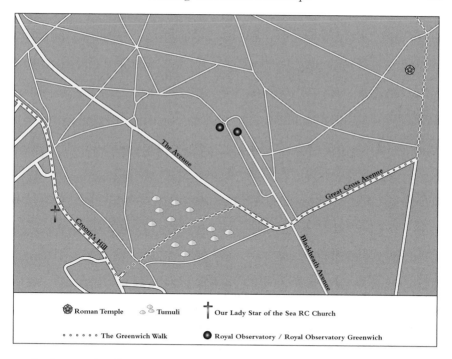

Roman Temple   Tumuli   Our Lady Star of the Sea RC Church

The Greenwich Walk   Royal Observatory / Royal Observatory Greenwich

19 The Greenwich walk

small area of grass, enclosed by railings, which is known locally as the Point. Until the nineteenth century, the Point was known as Maidenstone Hill. It is part of the chalk escarpment which runs from Shooters Hill towards London. Watling Street, the Roman Road from Canterbury to London, ran along this ridge of high ground, before descending to Southwark. This is also the route of a Celtic track which ran from Canterbury to St Albans. The Point is a curious place. According to some of the more fanciful works on early London, a stone circle once stood here, but there is not a scrap of evidence for such a thing. The view of London across the nearby rooftops is spectacular, as may be seen from *figure 20*. We are, in effect, standing on the edge of a cliff here; an unusual experience indeed in London!

Beneath the ground here is the series of caves known as Jack Cade's caverns or Blackheath caverns. These are almost certainly of prehistoric origin and were discovered accidentally in 1780. Photographs taken inside, when they were reopened briefly in 1938, indicate that they are a Dene Hole. These bell-shaped caves are found throughout south-east England and Jack Cade's caverns are fairly typical examples. Dene Holes were dug in chalk in prehistoric times, chiefly in Kent. They were probably chalk mines; the chalk being used to improve the quality of agricultural land. Flint can also be obtained from chalk mines and it is perhaps the case that these caves provided both these very useful materials. These caves are unusual in that they contain both a well and also a carving on the wall of a horned god, possibly Cernunnos. A similar but much smaller carved chalk image

20 The view from the Point

of a goddess was found in Grime's Graves, a chalk mine in Norfolk. There has been extensive mining for chalk in this area, right up to modern times. A consequence of this is that the appearance of large holes in roads is not unknown. Because, as we have seen, even so functional an activity as mining was seen in a religious context, it is by no means impossible that this site was used for worship as well as the extraction of minerals.

We retrace our steps now and enter Greenwich Park by the Croom's Hill Gate, which is on our right as we head back down Croom's Hill. The path ahead leads to grass, with a few trees scattered here and there. Unless one knew what to look for, it would be entirely possible to miss one of the most interesting pieces of London's ritual landscape which may still be seen more or less as it was created. On either side of the path are hillocks and bumps in the grass. Close examination reveals that these are round, like inverted saucers. *Colour plate 12* shows a typical example. In fact, these are round barrows; burial mounds from the Bronze Age. Actually, they are even more interesting than that. These early Bronze Age barrows, which were dug in the chalk, were reused over a thousand years later by the non-Christian Saxons. Greenwich is a Saxon settlement and they obviously recognised the barrows here as a burial ground. This is yet another example of continuity of use of a sacred place.

At first glance, these barrows or tumuli do not look at all impressive. They are, though, only the last remaining examples of what was once a huge chain of these monuments stretching from Kent to London. Others are still scattered in odd locations within a few miles of these ones. A little west of Greenwich, near Woolwich Common, is the only surviving barrow of a group of seven. The others were razed during building work some years ago. It is to be found at the junction of Shrewsbury Lane and Brinklow Crescent. A mile away, on Winn's Common, lies another tumulus, almost invisible in the shaggy grass.

The barrows in Greenwich Park must have looked startling at one time. Because of the geology of this area, one does not need to dig deep before striking chalk. These mounds were perhaps shining white when first completed and would have been visible for miles around. We continue walking towards the building ahead, which is a planetarium. Skirting round this and carrying on in the same direction, we pass the bandstand on our right, before coming to a small area enclosed by iron railings. This is all that remains of the Romano-Celtic temple complex which once dominated the road to Londinium. *Colour plate 7* shows what it would have looked like in its heyday, when it stood beside Watling Street, one of the main roads leading to the city of Londinium. All that now remains is a small block of mortar with brick tesserae embedded in it. At one time, it was thought that this might have been a Roman villa, but the discovery of coins and parts of a statue have shown it to have been a temple. As mentioned earlier, the arm of a female figure holding a long, rod-like object have been found here. The best guess is that this was a cult figure of Diana, goddess of the hunt. This shrine was the first building which one encounter when arriving at Londinium from Canterbury or Dover. The road which runs alongside the park here, in the opposite direction from which we came, is called Maze Hill. There was once a turf maze here, traces of which may be seen when the grass is parched. If we walk back to the planetarium and turn right, the hills by the Royal Observatory will lead back to Greenwich High Road and the station.

From the Source of the Walbrook to the Thames

We start this walk at Shoreditch High Street railway station. Leaving the station, we walk along Bethnal Green Road, taking the third turning on the left, Club Row, which takes us to the site of Friars' Mount, which is now the large, circular garden called Arnold Circus. *Figure 6* shows what this area looks like now.

There is something of a mystery about this public garden. The Walbrook rises from several sources a little to the north of the City of London. In prehistoric

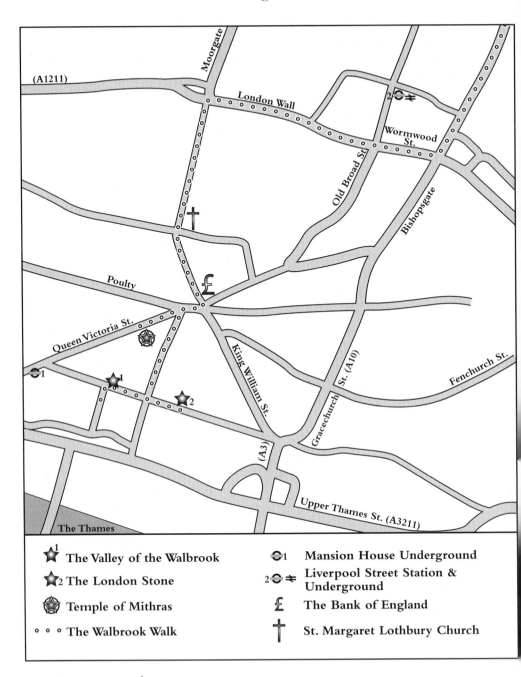

The Valley of the Walbrook ⭐1

⭐2 The London Stone

Temple of Mithras

° ° ° The Walbrook Walk

🔵1   Mansion House Underground

2🔵 ⇥   Liverpool Street Station &
Underground

£   The Bank of England

✝   St. Margaret Lothbury Church

21 The Walbrook walk

times, this was all marshland and the name of the Moorgate district reflects this. One of the principle springs which merged to become the Walbrook started near St Leonard's church in Shoreditch. In addition to the spring itself, there were two other notable features in this part of London. One was a sacred well; the so-called holy well. This well gave its name to the Augustinian priory which was founded nearby in what is now Holywell Lane. The Holywell priory was built on the site of the original holy well, almost certainly a case of the Christian church appropriating a pre-existing sacred site. Near to the well was an artificial mound called simply the Mount. It later became known as Friars' Mount, by association with the monastery. The Mount was probably another example of a Tothill such as was raised on Thorney Island and it may or may not still exist.

In the late nineteenth century, this part of Shoreditch had become a slum known as the Old Nichol. It covered much of the area between Old Street and Brick Lane and had become so notorious as a rookery or slum district that eventually it was swept away in a huge development of houses and flats for the working classes. Much of this redevelopment centred upon the site of Friars' Mount and a public garden was planted where Friars' Mount once stood. This garden is still there; it is called Arnold Circus and it is where we now stand. It will be seen at once that the garden at Arnold Circus is in fact a large mound; it is about 15ft tall. Alfred Watkins, whose ideas about ley lines we encountered in the last chapter, believed this to be the original prehistoric mound of Friars' Mount and incorporated it into one of his ley lines. There is, however, some doubt as to whether this is really the remains of Friars' Mount at all. During a dig in 2009, the Museum of London discovered that a good deal of this mound was composed of rubble from the demolition of the Old Nichol slum. The suspicion was that it had all been piled into a heap and then planted with trees and flowers. In short, far from being a pre-Roman mound, this was no more than a massive Victorian rubbish dump.

There is a question mark about this explanation though, which seems to leave open the possibility that part at least of the garden at Arnold Circus is genuinely ancient. If thousands of old bricks, pieces of old tile and cartloads of builders' rubble were to be piled 15ft high and a layer of gravel spread over the heap, it would not really be a fertile environment for planting trees and bushes, nor for establishing flower beds. And yet, as may readily be seen by glancing around, this mound seems to be covered with trees and bushes. In the centre of the garden, where there is a tarmac surface and a bandstand, there may well be some nineteenth-century hardcore, but the bulk of the mound is made up of earth.

It might be unwise to attach to much attention to the legends and lore of primary school children, but before undertaking their excavation, Museum of London staff asked local residents how much they knew about the raised garden. Children in nearby flats believed that an ancient king was buried beneath the mound with a hoard of treasure. Far fetched as it might be, one is tempted to wonder if this could be a genuine folk memory of a barrow grave. Still with the lore of schoolchildren, something like a taboo is attached to this mound. There is a school nearby and plenty of families, but one never sees children playing here. Some parents do not like the place and forbid their children to enter the garden.

Whatever its origins, there is something a little other worldly about the Arnold Circus garden. There is certainly nothing like it anywhere else in London and it is hard to avoid the suspicion that this might indeed be the remains of some sort of mound dating from before the Roman occupation. As we shall see, there is a slight trace of the Thorney Island Tothill, amounting to little more than a slight rise in the ground. It is by no means inconceivable that the slums of Old Nichol were built over Friars' Mount, which was revealed once more during the demolition.

Leaving Arnold Circus by Calvert Avenue, we arrive at Shoreditch High Street and then turn left. The church on our right, just before we turn into the High Street, is St Leonard's. This is one of the churches whose bells feature in the nursery rhyme *Oranges and Lemons*. We are now heading south along the route of Ermine Street, a major Roman road which led from London to Lincoln. The fourth turning on the right is Holywell Lane, where the priory used to be. The holy well itself was also somewhere in this vicinity. There can be little doubt that this area once formed part of the ritual landscape to the north of the Thames. A prehistoric mound, a holy well, boggy land and a spring all suggest this. When we see that a Christian religious house has been built over the top of this spot and the very name of the holy well adopted by the church, this practically clinches the matter. Walking down towards the City of London, we come first to Shoreditch and the Bishopsgate. The Walbrook runs alongside to our right, flowing under Liverpool Street station. The area around the station was a huge Roman graveyard which lay just north of Londinium and stretched as far as Spitalfields. In 1999, an elaborate Roman coffin was found there.

Shortly after passing Liverpool Street station on the right, we come to Camomile Street on the left and Wormwood Street on the right, which leads on to London Wall. This was where Ermine Street left Londinium. There was a gate in the city wall at this point. We turn right at this point into Wormwood Street and walk along until we rejoin the Walbrook as it flowed under the wall at Moorgate. It was near here that many skulls were recovered from the bed of the river in the nineteenth century. In addition to human skulls, many face pots have also been found in the valley of the Walbrook. Almost all the complete examples known come from this area. Turning left into Moorgate, we walk above the course of the river towards the Bank of England. When we reach Lothbury, we turn left and find the church of St Margaret's Lothbury. The vaults of this church were built over the Walbrook. Crossing the road, we arrive at the Bank of England. We are now in the valley of the Walbrook and the river still flows beneath our feet. During building works at the Bank of England, the Walbrook was seen flowing beneath the basement. Across the road is Mansion House, the official residence of the Lord Mayor of London. This too sits immediately above the course of the Walbrook, another curious instance of important buildings in the capital being located above old rivers.

Leading east is Cornhill, which was one of the two hills upon which Roman London was founded. The basilica was on Cornhill; it is now buried beneath Leadenhall Market. In the opposite direction, Cheapside points the way to Ludgate Hill. On the bank of the Walbrook near here stood a temple dedicated to Mithras. Mithraism, which had its roots in Persia, was a religion popular with Roman soldiers. Curiously, it was very much concerned with the death of a horned animal, a bull, whose sacrificial blood brought salvation. We have encountered this motif of the horned animal so often that it should not really come as a surprise that a cult in London had at its heart the death of a bull. When this temple was discovered during building work in 1954, it created a sensation. Crowds queued for hours in order to view the archaeological site. It was hoped to preserve the building in situ, but this proved impossible. It was moved a few hundred yards to Victoria Street, which runs south-west from Mansion House. It is worth visiting; the only temple to be excavated in the city.

Walking a few yards down Victoria Street brings us to the temple of Mithras on the left. The placing of the temple on this elevated site is unfortunate. *Colour plates 3 & 4* show the temple of Mithras as it was laid out after removal from its original location. As can be seen, it could hardly be a more public place, which could not be more different from how this temple would have been when it was in use. In fact, it was sunk into the ground and very gloomy and dark inside. Although this is the only temple discovered in London, there is a suspicion that the lower valley of the Walbrook near here was a religious area, with the banks of the stream being perhaps lined with temples and shrines.

Returning to Mansion House, we walk down Walbrook. This street runs parallel with the river, which is about a hundred yards to the right and heading in the same direction that we are. Halfway along this street on the right hand side was where the temple of Mithras was originally found. When we reach Cannon Street, we pause for a moment. To the right, there is a perceptible dip in Cannon Street, marking the place where the river crosses the street towards the Thames. It is very easy to see when looking up and down Cannon Street that this is a river valley. *Figure 22* gives some idea of the slope down to the Walbrook valley which is visible here. We turn left and walk up Cannon Street for a short distance. Set in the wall of an empty shop is an unremarkable piece of white stone. This is the London Stone and it has a very long history. *Figure 23* shows all that can be seen of the London Stone now. According to some legends, this is part of an altar to Diana from a temple built by the Trojan prince Brutus which supposedly stood on Ludgate Hill. A more probably theory is that it is a Roman milestone, from which distances to the city were measured. What is certain is that it has been a part of the London scene for at least a thousand years and possibly twice as long.

22 The bank of the Walbrook in Cannon Street

23 The London Stone (*Lonpicman/Wikimedia Commons*)

We retrace our steps and cross Walbrook, heading for the dip in the road which marks the course of the Walbrook. We cross Cannon Street and then walk into Cloak Lane. 'Cloak' is a corruption of the Latin *cloaca*, meaning sewer, which gives us an idea of how the Walbrook was treated by the time that it had reached this far in its journey to the Thames. If we walk to the Thames embankment, it is possible actually to see the Walbrook discharging into the Thames about a hundred yards to the west of Cannon Street railway station. It is only possible to see this at low tide. We can now walk back to Cannon Street tube and railway station.

On the Banks of the Fleet

We begin this walk at Angle tube station. Walk down Upper Street for a short distance and turn right into Pentonville Road. It may not feel like it, because the area is so built up that one cannot obtain a clear view, but you are now in one of the highest parts of central London. The first turning on the left as we walk up the Pentonville Road is called Mylne Street and this is a clue as to our whereabouts. The grassy mound on the left, just after Mylne Street, is now a covered reservoir.

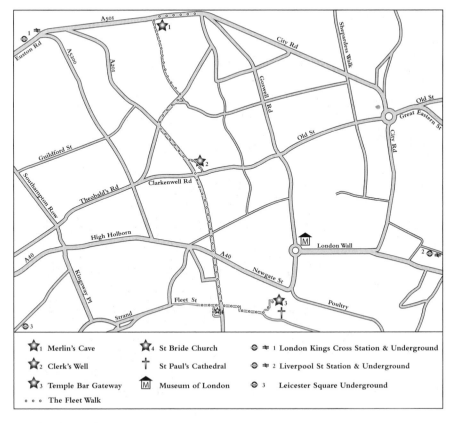

★1 Merlin's Cave	★4 St Bride Church	☮ ✠ 1 London Kings Cross Station & Underground
★2 Clerk's Well	† St Paul's Cathedral	☮ ✠ 2 Liverpool St Station & Underground
★3 Temple Bar Gateway	Ⓜ Museum of London	☮ 3 Leicester Square Underground
∘ ∘ ∘ The Fleet Walk		

24 The Fleet walk

It was once a cave, known as Merlin's Cave. Mylne Street was once Merlin Street. On the opposite side of the street from Merlin's Cave was a maze.

We continue walking and turn left into Amwell Street. This leads to Rosebery Avenue, where we turn right. There were many wells in this part of London, due to the proximity of the River Fleet. The Sadlers Wells theatre is in Rosebery Avenue. It is named after a famous well, which may still be seen beneath the theatre. Turn left at Farringdon Road and then turn left again after a short distance into Farringdon Lane, which runs parallel with Farringdon Road. On the left-hand side is a modern office building called Well Court. Peering through the window here, we are able to see the original Clerks' Well, which gave its name to this entire district, Clerkenwell. As may be seen from *figure 25*, this is not particularly impressive now. It is possible to arrange with Islington Council to inspect the well more closely and a telephone number is displayed on the door for those who are keen to do this. This was a holy well on the banks of the Fleet. It became enclosed by a nunnery in the twelfth century. There were three monasteries and nunneries on this section of the Fleet's course, suggesting that this was a sacred area before the coming of Christianity. The Clerks' Well became lost and was only rediscovered during building work in 1924.

Continue along Farringdon Lane. Look up Clerkenwell Green as you pass it on the left. It is very clear here that the land slopes down towards Farringdon Road. This is actually the river bank. Turn right and then left into Farringdon Road.

25 The Clerks' Well

26 Holborn Viaduct

The River Fleet flows beneath Farringdon Road and we shall follow its course down to another holy well near Fleet Street. As you walk along, look down the little side streets and alleyways leading off on either side. It is easy now to realise that we are actually in a valley. When we reach Holborn Viaduct, this becomes even more obvious. *Figure 26* looks just like a bridge, which in a sense is precisely what it is.

The viaduct, built between 1863 and 1869, carries traffic above us like a bridge, linking Holborn with Newgate Street. Holborn is an abbreviation of 'Hole Bourne', which is an old name for this section of the River Fleet. It was built because the streets leading down from Holborn towards the Fleet valley were so steep that horse-drawn buses had difficulty negotiating them. As we walk south, we pass St Bride Street on the right, named after the Christian saint who assumed the identity of the goddess Bride or Brigantia. We turn right into Fleet Street and cross the road. This was the Roman Akeman Street and led to the west of Britain. St Bride's church is tucked away behind the buildings and is reckoned by some to be the most beautiful church Christopher Wren ever designed. In the crypt, it is possible to view a small section of red tesserae pavement from a Roman building.

Figure 27 is of the Roman floor beneath St Bride's. This is almost certainly the only remaining part of a Romano-Celtic temple which once stood here. A holy well, dedicated to Bride existed in this area and was probably a cult centre for Briget.

Wells devoted to Bride were often thought to be a cure for infertility and there is another curious connection with this place and modern traditions. The design of the steeple (*colour plate 14*) was used in the eighteenth century as the model for wedding cakes. This type of multi-tiered cake is still in use today. It is strange that

27a A portion of Roman tesserae flooring beneath the church of St Bride's church (*with kind permission of St Bride's*)

27b A further portion of Roman tesserae flooring beneath the church of St Bride's church (*with kind permission of St Bride's*)

at so many weddings, the couple are unwittingly displaying a copy of the latest incarnation of a temple devoted to the pagan goddess Brigantia.

On leaving St Bride's, we cross Fleet Street and turn left, walking up to the church of St Dunstans. In the vestibule stand three statues. They are meant to represent the legendary King Lud and his sons. It will be remembered that Geoffrey of Monmouth thought that London was named after this mythical king. These figures stood on top of the Lud Gate, which stood on the same spot as the Roman gate. In 1760, the gate was demolished and the statues of Lud and his sons were taken by the Marquis of Hertford, who used them to decorate his garden in Regent's Park. They were brought here when St Dunstan's was rebuilt in 1829. We walk back to Ludgate Circus. The road slopes down perceptibly as we approach Ludgate Circus. This is because we are now walking down towards the valley of the Fleet River, which flowed at right angles to our path. We cross Farringdon Road and walk up Ludgate Hill. In Roman times, a bridge stood here, necessary to cross the Fleet. The Fleet was quite a large river at this point, not a mere stream like the Walbrook; the mouth of the Fleet when it entered the Thames was 600ft wide. This was one of the three hills upon which the Romans built their city of Londinium. It is only a gentle rise, but was dry land compared to the mudflats and marshes which covered most of the City of London at that time.

On the left, we pass Old Bailey, which leads to the Central Criminal Court, often called by the name of the street in which it is situated. There was a gate in the Roman city wall at this point. Crossing the road will take us to Pilgrim Street. Walk down a few yards and look at the corner on your right. A grimy block of white stone protects the corner wall of the building from traffic. This is the last surviving part of the old Lud Gate which once stood here. Walking to the top of the hill brings us to St Paul's Cathedral itself. A temple stood on or near to the cathedral when the Romans occupied this area and there is reason to suppose that it was dedicated to Diana, goddess of the hunt. The top of this hill was used as a graveyard from the Bronze Age onwards. Not only the Romans and Saxons used this place; a Viking tombstone has also been found and can be seen today in the Museum of London.

Walk a little further, to the left of the cathedral. Look up to your left and you will see a line of columns carrying what appear to be the heads of statues. This is a modern display, but it is intriguing to find the motif of the severed head so close to the cathedral. It is particularly curious since a few yards further, we come to Temple Bar, which once straddled Fleet Street and marked the point where Westminster and the City of London met. In *colour plate 11* we can see how Temple Bar looks today, following its rebuilding next to St Paul's Cathedral. The heads of those executed for treason were displayed on spikes here until 1772. This may be part of a cult of the severed head which had its roots thousands of years earlier; similar displays were to be found at London Bridge from the Middle Ages onwards. Walking through Paternoster churchyard will take us to St Paul's tube station. Just across the road in Foster Lane, a Roman altar to Diana, was found in the nineteenth century.

Tower Hill and Southwark

We start at Tower Hill tube station. It will be recalled that by some accounts this was the last resting place for the head of Bran. There is legend that Brutus, the Trojan prince that some still believe founded London and gave his name to the country of Britain, is buried here. An Iron Age burial was discovered on Tower Hill and there was once a sacred spring here which supposedly had healing qualities. This may have been a branch of the River Walbrook. This was also the eastern-most limit of the walls of Londinium. A well-preserved stretch of the Roman wall can still be seen in Coopers Row. We cross Coopers Row to Trinity Green. At the west end of this garden is a commemorative plaque, marking the spot where the beheadings took place from the fourteenth to eighteenth centuries. Leaving Trinity Green, we cross Trinity Square and walk up Muscovy Street until reaching Seething Lane. Turn right and in a short distance we find the gateway of St Olave's church on our left. This gateway is decorated with five larger than life size stone skulls. *Figure 13* is of this strange entrance to a Christian place of worship. This seems to be a motif for this part of London: the skull or decapitated head. St Olave's church is perhaps built upon the site of an earlier pagan shrine. A carving

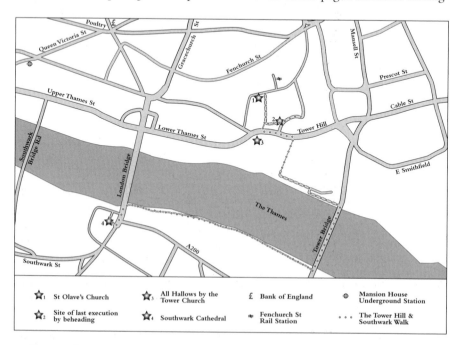

| ⭐₁ St Olave's Church | ⭐₃ All Hallows by the Tower Church | £ Bank of England | ◉ Mansion House Underground Station |
| ⭐₂ Site of last execution by beheading | ⭐₄ Southwark Cathedral | ⚓ Fenchurch St Rail Station | ∘∘∘ The Tower Hill & Southwark Walk |

28 Tower Hill and Southwark walk

was found near here which showed three Roman mother goddesses, which was possibly part of an altar. Walk back down Seething Lane and straight ahead is the church of All Hallows by the Tower. This is the oldest church in London. Crossing the road, we enter the church. The crypt contains a mosaic floor from the second century AD. There is also Saxon masonry and an arch, the only examples of Saxon architecture in the whole of London. *Colour plate 8* shows this and the Roman tiles incorporated in the arch are clearly visible. The bodies of some of those who were decapitated on Tower Hill were brought to this church before burial. Leave the church and turn right. We come to a plaza on the right; this is Tower Hill itself. Looking down towards the Thames here makes us realise that we are actually at the summit of a hill, albeit a very modest one. Walking down towards the river, with the Tower on our left, we turn left at the bottom of the hill and then walk along the path towards Tower Bridge. We cross over the bridge and then turn right, walking along the riverside path. The bridge which we are approaching is the latest London Bridge. The Roman bridge across the river was near this spot. Large numbers of coins from the period have been found in the river here, suggesting an existing tradition of votive deposits here which was continued by the Romans. The idea of offering a sacrifice for being allowed by the spirits to cross a bridge or ford in safety is an old one. We see it in the story of the 'Three Billy Goats Gruff', where a nature spirit dwells beneath the bridge. He demands a blood sacrifice for any crossing of the bridge. In later times, coins were offered as a substitute.

There was a gatehouse at the entrance to the old London bridge and it was here that the heads of those decapitated at Tower Hill and other places were displayed. At one time, there were as many as 34 heads here and they were in the charge of a specially appointed Keeper of the Heads. It is hard to avoid the thought that here too was another manifestation of the cult of the head. Particularly since when a head started to decay and had been picked more or less clean by ravens, it was then cast into the Thames.

Climb the steps leading up to London Bridge and then cross the road. Turn left and walk away from the Thames. When you reach the pedestrian crossing before the railways bridge which crosses the road ahead, pause for a moment. You are standing near the summit of one of the small hills which were here before Londinium was built. Duke Street Hill, up which we are walking, was an island of gravel covered in brick earth which rose 20ft or so above the surrounding marshes. A barrow has been excavated on the slopes of this hill and a maze stood nearby in Tudor times. A few hundred yards to the south, along Borough High Street, was a Romano-Celtic temple complex which was dedicated to Mars-Camulos. The point where we are now standing was where Watling Street crossed the bridge and entered Londinium. The temples near here would be the second group which a traveller from the south would encounter. The first was at Greenwich, a temple of Diana. On our right is Southwark Cathedral. In order to reach the cathedral, though, it is necessary to descend a steep flight of steps.

Southwark is the least known of London's cathedrals. The Cathedral and Collegiate Church of St Saviour and St Mary Overie, to give it its full name, was only raised to cathedral status in 1905. The main part of the church dates from the early thirteenth century and it is the first gothic church built in London. There are several peculiarities about the church, which some have said could have a bearing upon the pagan origins of this site as a place of worship. For example, it is unique among British cathedrals in having no west door.

A well was investigated beneath the cathedral and found to contain a cult statue of a Romano-Celtic god. *Colour plate 15* and *figure 2* show this statue and may be seen if you walk through the cathedral into the new extension and conference room. Next to the case containing the god is a shaft leading down to the position of the Roman road which once passed here. A section of the Roman road may be seen. When the well was investigated, traces of a roman building were also found. If you return to the cathedral itself, you will find a small section of the Roman tesserae from the building in the south aisle. This is shown in the upper photograph in *colour plate 10*. It is not known whether this building was a domestic house or a temple. The presence of the god in the disused well could indicate that this was a sacred site for the Celts and later Romans.

A short distance from here was the Tabard Inn, mentioned in Chaucer's *Canterbury Tales* as a popular starting point for the pilgrimage to Beckett's tomb. This was part of a religious contract in medieval times, whereby pilgrims made the journey in exchange for a favour from God. They purchased badges at Canterbury Cathedral and many threw them into the Thames on their return to prove that they had fulfilled their part of the contract with the gods. London Bridge rail and tube station can be reached now by retracing our steps and crossing the road.

Thorney Island

We begin by the Houses of Parliament, overlooking the river. The nearest tube station is Westminster. There was a ford from this point and at low tide it is still almost possible to walk across the riverbed. It was here, according to legend, that King Canute failed to halt the incoming tide. Cross the road to St Margaret's church and then walk past it, following the road round to Westminster Abbey. *Minster* is simply and old English word meaning a large church which was once part of a monastery; York Minster is another example. This one was called Westminster to distinguish it from St Paul's in the city, which was once known as the East Minster. There has been a church on this site since Saxon times. Before that, there was probably a Roman temple which was perhaps sacred to Apollo. In the abbey is displayed a Roman sarcophagus, dug up here in 1869. Other Roman burials have been found in Westminster, the most recent at the church of St Martin-in-the-Fields. Some archaeologists are now speaking of Roman Westminster; an acknowledgement

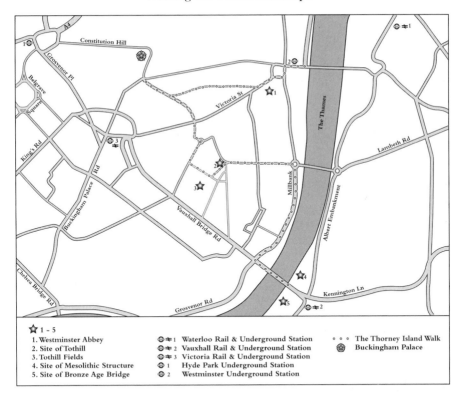

29 Thorney Island walk

that there was a definite Roman presence in this area. Following the most ancient traditions, it is here that monarchs of Britain are anointed and crowned. The ecclesiastical status of Westminster Abbey is a little odd. It is what is known as a 'Royal Peculiar'. This means that the church and its clergy answer only to the monarch; they are not under the jurisdiction of any bishop.

The square of grass between the Abbey and Great Smith Street is called Dean's Yard. There was a sacred spring here which later became known as the holy well. All traces of it have now disappeared. We are now standing on Thorney Island, the smaller of the two islands formed by the delta of the Tyburn and the most sacred. If we now cross over Victoria Street, we come to Tothill Street. This road commemorates the mound of Tothill which stood nearby for many years. This road is perfectly aligned with the nave of Westminster Abbey. Walking along Tothill Street, which becomes Broadway and then Petty France, we come to Buckingham Palace gate. If we turn right and walk up for a few yards, we will see the palace in front of us.

Buckingham Palace is built directly over the Tyburn. It is still possible to walk along the bed of the Tyburn from the Thames and find oneself beneath the palace. It is built upon what would have been the northernmost tip of the larger of the two islands which made up Thorney Island. It is indeed curious that parliament, the legislature of the nation, the greatest church and also the residence of the royal family should all have ended up on Thorney Island.

Walking back down Buckingham Palace gate and then crossing Victoria Street again, we walk down Artillery Row. Turning left, right and then second left, brings us into Vincent Square. The playing fields which we see here are all that now remains of Tothill Field. It was here that there was a maze and also where the Game of Troy was played. At the end of Vincent Square, we turn left into Maunsel Street, which brings us to the junction of Regency Street. Just before you reach Regency Street, look at the houses on the left hand side. You will see that they are a little higher as you move forward. This is the spot where the Tothill stood, before Westminster was almost completely built over. This almost imperceptible rise in the ground is all that is left of the Tothill. If you stand in Regency Street and look at the shop on the corner of Maunsel Street, you can also see a slight rise. Often, as we have seen, the only remaining sign of London's rivers or sacred sites amounts to no more than this, a slight rise or dip in the level of a street.

Continue walking in the same direction and the main road is Horseferry Road. There really was a horse ferry across the Thames at the end of this road. Walking down Horseferry Road to the Thames, we arrive at the river and turn right, walking towards Vauxhall Bridge. Crossing over the bridge, turning right and walking a couple of hundred yards, we find ourselves at the site of the Bronze Age bridge or pier which we have discussed at length. All that may now be seen at high tide are a few wooden stumps. Even then, it is only at the lowest of tides that they are visible. Channel 4's *Time Team* conducted an exploration of this site in 1999 and it is as a result of this that we now know the age of this enigmatic structure.

Looking across the Thames, it is possible to see the outfall from the Tyburn, which is now only a sewer. The course of the river has changed over the years; nobody is quite sure when or why. The River Effra also entered the Thames at this point and in the direction in which we are now looking was probably an island, connected both to Thorney Island and this bank of the Thames by the wooden bridge. If the arrangement was anything at all like Flag Fen or La Tène, there may well have been a wooden platform on the island to enable those making the pilgrimage to this spot to make their offerings to the world of the spirits.

Walk back to Vauxhall Bridge and then carry on along the river bank. The futuristic building on the right is the headquarters of MI6, the British Secret Intelligence Service. At very low spring tides, the remains of wooden posts may be seen in the mud of the Thames foreshore immediately in front of the MI6 headquarters. These only came to light in 2010. Be very careful if photographing these 6000-year old piles. When an archaeological survey was conducted here in 2010, a member of the public dialled 999 on the grounds that a group of men were preparing to launch shoulder-fired missiles at MI6! A team of armed police arrived and discovered only tripods which were used in surveying and measuring the remains. Walking back over Vauxhall Bridge will take you to Pimlico tube station.

11

Conclusion

We have in this book explored a lost world; the rivers and hills of a prehistoric land which vanished thousands of years ago. That traces of this forgotten country may still be discerned beneath the capital is unknown to most of those who now live in the London. An attempt has been made to deduce various things about our ancestors from examining what is left of their culture. It is perhaps time to strike a note of caution.

Extrapolating from meagre physical remains such as those at which we have looked and trying to reconstruct the belief systems of men and women who have been dead for millennia is, at best, a chancy and uncertain enterprise. Museums are full of mundane items of everyday use which were once labelled 'Ritual Objects'. We regularly designate any rectangular hut found in an Iron Age British setting as a 'temple'. This is simply because such structures are different from the round houses in which most people seemingly lived. Without further evidence, it is impossible to say if we are on the right track; these little square buildings might, for all we know to the contrary, have been communal tool sheds!

This process of possible misunderstanding of what we unearth can also work in the opposite direction. We saw that until recently, bronze weapons fished out of the Thames were thought to have been lost or mislaid. Ritual shafts into the underworld were once dismissed as rubbish dumps. It may very well be the case that in the future, an entirely new and wholly different explanation will be advanced, more satisfying than either of those which have been so far suggested. This is because archaeology is not a static body of knowledge but a living and constantly changing discipline. If this were not the case, then we would still be content to believe that the world was created 6000 years ago and that Neolithic arrow heads are made by the fairies. Our idea about the past are changing all the time and this is a good and healthy thing.

I have interpreted the evidence which is freely available to everybody in a particular way. It is inevitable that some of the ideas which have been explored here will turn out to be mistaken or distorted. After all, it is only in the last 20 years or so that the wooden structures at Vauxhall have been discovered and the trackways across the marshes of south London. New discoveries are bound to turn current ideas on their head in the future. Nevertheless, it is unlikely that the core idea of this book will be exploded; that there was in London for thousands of years before the coming of the Romans, a cult centre which was the object of pilgrimage from other parts of the country. It may well be the case that I am mistaken about the precise nature of the deities involved in this cult or about the practices which were connected with it, but that some species of cult or religion was centred upon this part of the Thames valley seems to be a racing certainty.

Scientists, when examining an hypothesis, often apply an intellectual tool known as Occam's razor. This medieval aphorism suggests that we should always adopt the simplest explanation which meets all the known facts. I have been guided by this principle when looking at the early history of London. For example when tens of thousands of worked flints are dredged from the River Thames, as happened during Victorian gravel dredging operations, there are a number of explanations for how those flint axes found their way into the river. By far and away the simplest of the possible explanations is that they were put in the water deliberately. All that I have done is work through the evidence, trying to follow in a sense the line of least resistance by always choosing what appears to me to be the simplest explanation for what is seen. The result has been the present book.

I hope that readers who live in or near London will be prompted to visit the sites which have been talked about here. There are still plenty of remains to be found; literally laying on the ground. The Mesolithic wooden structure in front of the MI6 Headquarters for instance, has simply been sitting on the Thames foreshore for 6000 years until somebody in 2010 realised its significance. Even a simple stroll along the shore of the Thames at low tide can reveal flint weapons and tools. Visits to museums such as the Museum of London and British Museum will also be rewarding for those with an interest in the early history of London.

The story of London is not a simple, clear cut and straight narrative, such as one might find in a children's history book. Instead it is a complicated, murky and confusing legend, in which each succeeding generation tries to interpret the ancient past in the light of their own culture and value system. This book has been only the latest such attempt to make sense of what has been seen. It is inevitable that there will be others in the future which will make a better job of the task. All we can say is that at present, nothing in the archaeological record contradicts the theses which I have advanced and that the story which I have outlined has at least as much chance of being the correct one as any other.

Bibliography

Alcock, Joan (1996) *Life in Roman Britain*, London, B.T. Batsford

Ashe, Geoffrey (1990) *Mythology of the British Isles*, London, Methuen

Ashley, Peter (2007) *More London Peculiars*, Swindon, English Heritage

Bahn, Paul (ed.) (1996) *Tombs, Graves and Mummies*, London, George Weidenfield & Nicolson

Bedoyere, Guy de la (2006) *Roman Britain: A New History*, London, Thames & Hudson

Birley, Anthony (1964) *Life in Roman Britain*, London, B.T. Batsford

Brandon, David & Brooke, Alan (2006) *London the Executioner's City*, Stroud, Sutton Publishing

Clayton, Antony (2008) *The Folklore of London*, London, Historical Publications

———— (2000) *Subterranean London*, London, Historical Publications

Cunliffe, Barry (1993) *The Roman Baths at Bath*, Bath, Bath Archaeological Trust

———— (2010) *Druids*, Oxford, Oxford University Press

d'Este, Sorita (ed.) (2008) *Horns of Power*, London, Avalonia

Davies, Hunter (1983) *A Walk Round London's Parks*, London, Hamish Hamilton

Delaney, Frank (1986) *The Celts*, London, Hodder & Stoughton

Dyer, James (1990) *Ancient Britain*, London, B.T. Batsford

Flanders, Judith (ed.) (1998) *Mysteries of the Ancient World*, London, Weidenfield & Nicolson

Fraser, Antonia (1988) *Boadicea's Chariot*, London, Weidenfield & Nicolson

Frazer, James (1922) *The Golden Bough*, York, The Macmillan Co.

Frere, Sheppard (1967) *Brittania*, London, Routledge & Kegan Paul

Glinert, Ed (2003) *The London Compendium*, London, Allen Lane

Gordon, E.O. (1914) *Prehistoric London: its Mounds and Circles*, London, Covenant Publishing

Hole, Christina (1976) *British Folk Customs*, London, Hutchinson

Jenkins, Simon (1999) *England's Thousand Best Churches*, London, Penguin Books

Konstam, Angus (2001) *Historical Atlas of the Celtic World*, New York, Checkmark Books

Lewis, Spence (1998) *Mysteries of Celtic Britain*, Bristol, Parragon

Lewis-Williams, David & Pearce, David (2005) *Inside the Neolithic Mind*, London, Thames & Hudson

Long, David (2006) *Spectacular Vernacular*, Stroud, Sutton Publishing

Pryor, Francis (2003) *Britain B.C.*, London, Harper Collins

Renfrew, Colin (1987) *Archaeology and Language*, London, Jonathon Cape

Salway, Peter (1993) *A History of Roman Britain*, Oxford, Oxford University Press

Segal, Robert (2004) *Myth*, Oxford, Oxford University Press

Senior, Michael (1979) *Myths of Britain*, London, Guild Publishing

Sharkey, John (1975) *Celtic Mysteries*, London, Thames & Hudson

Sheuel, Brian (1985) *Traditional Customs of Britain*, Exeter, Webb & Bower

Shuckburgh, Julian (2003) *London Revealed*, London, Harper Collins

Smith, Stephen (2004) *Underground London*, London, Abacus

Tacitus, translated by Harold Mattingly (1948) *Agricola*, London, Penguin

Timpson, John (1993) *Timpson's Other England*, Norwich, Jarrold Publishing

Wacher, John (1978) *Roman Britain*, Stroud, J.M. Dent

Warner, Rex (1950) *Men and Gods*, London, MacGibbon & Kee

Williams, Brenda (2006) *Ancient Britain*, Andover, Jarrold Publishing

Young, Simon (2009) *The Celtic Revolution*, Gibson Square

Index

DAVID LONG

HIDDEN CITY

THE SECRET ALLEYS, COURTS & YARDS
OF LONDON'S SQUARE MILE

FOREWORD BY THE RT. HON. THE LORD MAYOR OF LONDON, ALDERMAN MICHAEL BEAR

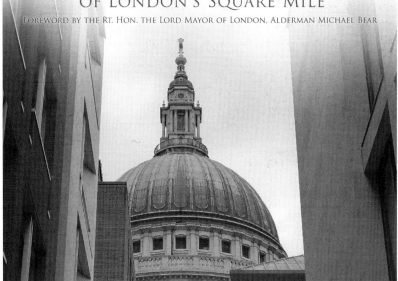

**HIDDEN CITY
THE SECRET ALLEYS, COURTS AND YARDS OF
LONDON'S SQUARE MILE**
by David Long

978 0 7524 5774 1

www.thehistorypress.co.uk

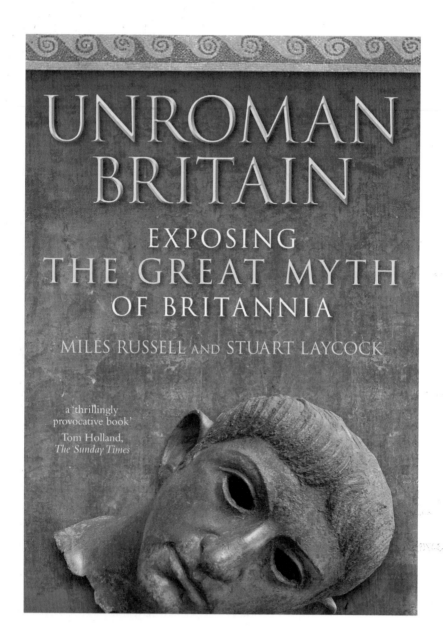

UNROMAN BRITAIN
EXPOSING THE GREAT MYTH OF BRITANNIA
by Miles Russell & Stuart Laycock

978 0 7524 6285 1

www.thehistorypress.co.uk